G
Ge
& Italian Riviera

Text by Susie Boulton
Photography by Neil Buchan-Grant
Design: Roger Williams
Series Editor: Tony Halliday

Berlitz® POCKET GUIDE

Genoa
& Italian Riviera

First Edition 2006

NO part of this book may be reproduced, stored in a retrieval system or transmitted in any form or means electronic, mechanical, photocopying, recording or otherwise, without prior written permission from Berlitz Publishing. Brief text quotations with use of photographs are exempted for book review purposes only.

PHOTOGRAPHY CREDITS
All pictures by Neil Buchan-Grant, except pages 15, 16 and 19 by akg-images London; page 64 by Mark Read
Cover picture: Neil Buchan-Grant

CONTACTING THE EDITORS
Every effort has been made to provide accurate information in this publication, but changes are inevitable. The publisher cannot be responsible for any resulting loss, inconvenience or injury. We would appreciate it if readers would call our attention to any errors or outdated information by contacting Berlitz Publishing, PO Box 7910, London SE1 1WE, England.
Fax: (44) 20 7403 0290;
e-mail: berlitz@apaguide.co.uk
www.berlitzpublishing.com

Bordighera (page 46), long a local favourite resort on the Riviera

Genoa's San Lorenzo Cathedral (page 26)

Baiardo (page 44) is one of several delightful inland hill villages

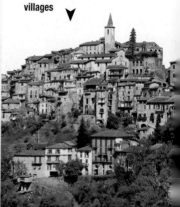

TOP TEN ATTRACTIONS

Corniglia (page 78) is the most remote village of the dramatic Cinque Terre ▼

The Aquarium (page 29) is a highlight among the sights in Genoa's renovated port area

◄

►

Strozzi's *The Cook* is part of the collection of paintings in the Palazzo Rosso, (page 32), one of Genoa's finest museums

Portofino (page 69), the quintessential resort of the Ligurian Riviera, has been attracting visitors for decades ▼

►

Alassio (page 54) has one of the best sandy beaches on the coast

Palm-filled Hanbury Gardens (page 41) beckons garden-lovers

►

Get up early to visit the famous flower market in San Remo (page 46)

►

CONTENTS

Fact Sheets

INTRODUCTION

Squeezed between sea and mountains, the Italian Riviera winds and twists in a long, thin arc from the French border in the west to Tuscany in the east. The name has a glamorous ring to it, conjuring up images of brilliant skies, shimmering seas and palm-fringed beaches. It was the dramatic natural beauty and the balmy winters that drew the first tourists here from the mid-19th century. In 1855 Giovanni Ruffini's romantic novel, *Doctor Antonio,* whose events take place on the Riviera, set the trend for well-heeled British and other northern Europeans to winter on the mild and flower-filled coast west of Genoa. Like the French Riviera, the coastline became a playground for northern European royalty and aristocrats; while to the east of Genoa the Gulf of Spezia, or Gulf of Poets as it later became known, inspired Byron, Shelley and other romantics.

The image may be familiar but few Europeans outside Italy can actually place Italy's Riviera. Most know of Genoa as a seaport and are familiar with the French Riviera to the west and Tuscany which borders the region to the east. But 'the other Riviera' or Liguria (as the region is officially known) has been comparatively neglected by foreign travellers.

Famous Mountains and Fine Flora

World War II inflicted severe damage on Genoa and many of the smaller ports; a rapid post-war economic recovery gave rise to a major building boom and expanded industries. Today the Riviera lacks the cachet of its French counterpart and cannot boast the art of neighbouring Tuscany. Nevertheless the region still preserves what made it famous: the

Picturesque Portovenere

mountains tumbling into deep blue seas, the equable climate and the abundance of plants. It also preserves a number of picturesque fishing villages, some fascinating medieval quarters and a glorious, unspoilt hinterland.

The region is neatly divided into two by Genoa, capital of Liguria. The city rises theatrically above the water, its houses, skyscrapers and suburbs stacked in tiers on the hillside. Birthplace of the explorer Christopher Columbus and the naval hero Andrea Dorea, the city has always been dominated by all things maritime. It grew rich on trade with the Orient, played a vital role in the Crusades and became a dominant power of the Mediterranean. By the end of the 13th century, the Genoese Empire extended as far as Constantinople (today's Istanbul) and Syria and might have ruled the Mediter-

Literary Links

Liguria has a long list of admirers among the literati. Although Dickens had mixed feelings about Genoa, and Leigh Hunt and Thomas Hardy wrote poems bewailing her loss of greatness, Flaubert described it as 'a city all in marble with gardens full of roses' and Thomas Gray, in 1739, wrote 'We find this place so fine, that we are in fear of finding nothing finer.' Byron and Shelley are immortalised in the Gulf of La Spezia where they took up residence. Byron swam 8km (5 miles) across the bay and Shelley drowned in a storm sailing back from Livorno. Shelley's wife, Mary Wollstonecraft, reputedly found her inspiration for *Frankenstein* at Lerici's castle, while the Bay of Fables at Sestri Levante was given its name by Hans Christian Andersen. Monet painted Bordighera and the medieval town of Dolceacqua, Hemingway stayed in Alassio and made his mark on the celebrated Muretto (Little Wall). A number of musicians found inspiration here, including Tchaikovsky, who completed *Eugene Onegin* in the Russian colony at San Remo, and Verdi, who wrote *Aida* in Genoa.

ranean were it not for the intense rivalry with Venice. In the Battle of Chioggia in 1380 the Venetians defeated the Genoese Navy, winning undisputed maritime supremacy in the Mediterranean and leading to the decline of Genoa. In the early 16th century, when Columbus opened up American trade routes for the Spanish Empire, he altered the whole pattern of world trade, ironically stifling western expansion for his native city.

Genoese lion

Though rich in history, Genoa is not a city which readily endears itself to tourists. It is, after all, the largest seaport in Italy, with kilometres of docks and a reputation as a traffic-choked and rough-edged place. But there is much more to Genoa than first meets the eye. Behind the industrial sprawl lies an atmospheric labyrinth of medieval alleys, ancient monuments and museums, and many mansions and palazzi of mercantile families, some of them housing rich collections of art.

Genoa's Old Port and the Two Rivieras

In an effort to rid itself of its seamy image Genoa transformed its Porto Antico (Old Port) for Expo 1992, celebrating the quincentenary of Christopher Columbus' 1492 voyage. The former port of warehouses, funnels and factories is now a leisure and cultural centre, with Europe's largest aquarium, a portside promenade, a large maritime museum and plenty of other waterside attractions for visitors.

To the west of Genoa lies the Riviera di Ponente (Coast of the Setting Sun) and to the east the Riviera di Levante (Coast of the Rising Sun). While the western Riviera has an almost uninterrupted string of resorts, the cliffs and mountains east of Genoa have precluded major development and you can still find chic resorts and cliffhanging villages where multi-coloured houses overlook tiny coves of limpid seas. Protected by the Ligurian and Maritime Alps, both coasts provide shelter from northern winds. The flora is abundant and wherever you go the air is scented with citrus and almond blossom. In other respects the coasts are very different.

Along the western Riviera you might assume a continuation of the French Riviera. All the natural features are here, the rugged hills stretching into mountains and valleys, corniche roads and splendid vistas of land and sea, but there the comparison ends. The resorts as you come over the border are less pristine and sophisticated, more noisy and laid back. This is a busy, bustling and very Italian holiday area, where scooters hurtle along the main Via Aurelia, resorts are frequently cut off from beaches by the road and railway, and the sands are hidden under regimented rows of parasols and deckchairs.

On the plus side there is more variety of landscape than the French Riviera and most towns preserve a medieval quarter where you can stroll along narrow alleys or linger over a glass of local wine in a little café or bar.

> **The Ligurian coastlines vie for the most evocative epithet. Apart from the Riviera di Ponente (Coast of the Setting Sun) and the Riviera di Levante (Coast of the Rising Sun), there are the Riviera dei Fiori (Coast of the Flowers), Riviera delle Palme (Coast of the Palms), Golfo Paradiso (Paradise Gulf) and Golfo dei Poeti (Gulf of the Poets). In some cases, the romance of the names is now outweighed by reality.**

A typical Riviera villa, at La Spezia

Grande-dame resorts such as San Remo and Bordighera retain some of the elegance of their heyday as fashionable resorts, and Albenga and Noli have beautiful medieval centres.

The Quieter Riviera di Levante

If you are looking for something quieter, head to the Riviera di Levante east of Genoa. The coast here has a more rugged and wild beauty, with rocky promontories and cliffs plunging sheer to the sea. Resorts are quieter, more picturesque and, in season, accessible by boat. Hopping on ferries from one port to the next is a delightful way of exploring the coast. Famous little Portofino, put on the map by a star-studded cast in the 1950s and 60s, still draws the international jet set – along with a huge number of day-trippers. The scenic highlight is the Cinque Terre, the ancient and formerly remote cliff villages, now accessible by all means of transport and inundated by tourists, but still undeniably picturesque.

The best of the beaches lie along the Riviera di Ponente, where a few resorts such as Alassio have wide, sandy bays. But more often than not beaches are disappointing patches of grey sand or shingle. Along the Riviera di Levante there are typically small pebbly or rocky stretches wherever cliffs and mountains permit. Often the best swimming is off the rocks or cliffs. Some of the little coves have gloriously clear aquamarine waters, ideal for scuba diving or snorkelling.

Italy's Hilliest Region

Liguria is the hilliest region in Italy, with two-thirds of the land occupied by mountains over 1,000m (3,300ft) high; it's

Mountain homes

also the most heavily wooded region. Lower slopes are planted with olives, vines and citrus groves, above them are pine, forests of sweet chestnut and oak, and higher still conifers and larch. Not far from the coast, mountain villages are perched high on hilltops or on steep slopes of wooded valleys. Some of the remote, higher villages are semideserted and their agricultural way of life abandoned for more lucrative pursuits in tourism along the coast. But where there is life, rural traditions are maintained, and time seems to stand still. It all seems a world apart from the populous resorts below.

A BRIEF HISTORY

The earliest evidence of human settlers in the region is a 230,000-year-old hip bone, discovered in the Balzi Rossi caves and displayed in the nearby museum. Skulls and tools of later Neanderthal man were also discovered here, along with skeletons, jewellery and 'Venus' figurines of *Homo sapiens sapiens* who sheltered in the same caves.

The region takes its name from the earliest known tribes from the first millennium BC, who inhabited a region from northwest Spain to northeast Italy. Their natural resource was the sea and they traded with the Phoenicians and Greeks, earning a reputation as freebooters and pirates. Evidence of the earliest Ligurian shepherds are the rock etchings of 1800–1000BC on the slopes of Monte Bego just across the border in France.

Romans and Lombards

Archaeological remains found at Genoa indicate that Greek settlers were living here from at least the 6th century BC. The Romans were slow in setting foot in the region, their progress continually impeded by the tough Ligurians. The fall of Genoa in the 2nd century BC was followed by the gradual Roman colonisation of the coast. Vital routes were constructed including the Via Julia Augusta (241BC) following the coast (the present-day Via Aurelia) and the Via Postumia from Medoilanum (Milan) to Genua (Genoa). Genoa, which allied itself to Rome, was destroyed by the Carthaginians in 205BC, but was soon rebuilt by the Romans. The whole region finally came under Roman rule by 180BC. Evidence of Roman occupation in the region is scanty: half an amphitheatre at Ventigmiglia, the remains of a cargo found in a sunken Roman galley and displayed in the naval museum at Albenga, the odd bridge and some sculptural fragments.

Following the breakdown of the Roman Empire in the West in AD476, Liguria was subject to the same waves of invaders as the rest of northern Italy. The Lombards, semi-nomadic, warfaring Norsemen, descended on the region in 568, putting an end to any vestige of political unity that may have survived the Roman era. In 643 they conquered Genoa, destroying the walls and allowing trade to decline. Eventually, however, they were absorbed into the Italian population, adopting Roman dress and law, speaking the local language and, in many cases, converting to Christianity. Little remains from their era, though the Christian baptistry at Albenga *(see page 57)* displays some features of Lombard architecture.

In the mid-8th century the pope appealed to the Christian Franks for support against the Lombards. Pepin, king of the Franks, sent forces into Italy and, in 774, his son Charlemagne completed his father's work by deposing the Lombard king, Desiderius. In 800 Charlemagne was crowned Holy Roman Emperor by Pope Leo. The Franks failed to establish a durable state in Italy, however, and the ensuing era of feudal anarchy was characterised by Saracen sieges.

The Communes

Liguria's medieval and Renaissance history, with its shifting power bases and allegiances, is so complex that no comprehensive Ligurian history has ever been written. The 19th-century historian Jacob Burkhardt was dismissive of Genoa: 'Party conflicts here assumed so fierce a character, and disturbed so violently the whole course of life, that we can hardly understand how, after so many revolutions and invasions, the Genoese ever contrived to return to an endurable condition'.

The Holy Roman emperors took less and less interest in Italian affairs, and this power vacuum led to one of the most politically important developments in medieval northern Italy: the rise of the communes, or free city states. Although

Genoese bankers in the late 14th century

by now all political unity bequeathed by Rome had long gone, much of its urban civilisation had survived. Many of the *municipie* (free cities) had become commercially prosperous, creating a situation in which local forces could set up autonomous cities, or *comuni*. These *comuni* were, however, vulnerable to factional and party feuds, with powerful families often grouping together in particular localities within the town walls. These groups, or *consortie,* built fortified towers often rising to great heights – the higher the tower, the more prestigious the family. The great ideological conflict between the papacy and the Holy Roman Empire gave further impetus to conflict when these 'superpowers' vied for support in the northern cities. Their supporters, sometimes whole cities, adopted the labels 'Guelph' for the papacy and 'Ghibelline' for the empire.

During the 13th century, factional, financial or intercity crises often led to the appointment of a *podestà*, a temporary dictator from outside a commune who was given a writ to deal with a crisis. As the towns sprouted up and the disputes grew in number, the podestà was replaced by a permanent warlord or leader of a powerful family or faction. By the 14th century these *'capitani'* were appointed to check the growing power of patricians and even more importantly, the individual despots or *'signori'*. This trend of emerging Communes was particularly relevant to Liguria.

Genoa's Golden Age

The paramount power in Liguria was Genoa. The city developed a war fleet following repeated Saracen invasions and

Genoa in 1493

the sacking of the city in 935. In 1097 Genoa contributed ten galleys to the First Crusade and in return received trading posts and privileges in the Levant. Business interests were also developed inland and Genoa produced innovators in shipbuilding, navigation, cartography and banking. Bitter rivalry and battles between Genoa and Pisa continued until the great naval Battle of Meloria (1284), when Genoa soundly defeated her neighbour, capturing 29 of her galleys and sinking seven. Pisa was never to recover from the defeat. By the end of the 13th century Genoa was master of Corsica and

Sardinia, with trading posts in Constantinople, Crimea, Syria, Cyprus and Tunis. In 1339, Simone Boccanegra was appointed *doge* (ruler) for life with absolute power.

As Genoa expanded from a trading commune in the 11th century to a formidable maritime commercial power in the 14th and 15th centuries, other Ligurian towns came under her dominion. Cities that had once enjoyed commune status were eclipsed by Genoa, and by the end of the 14th century Genoese rule stretched the length of Liguria.

Genoa's expansion abroad brought her into sharp conflict with Venice, the greatest European sea power of the time. By 1380, after constant wars and feuds, Genoa had come within an ace of entering Venice, but in that year it was defeated at the Battle of Chioggia. The battle and subsequent peace treaty (in 1381) marked the end of its role as a dominant power.

By the turn of the century, Genoa was oppressed by huge government debt. Creditors combined to form the Banco di San Giorgio, which secured so many privileges that it even began to rival the state and effectively controlled the city for much of the 15th century.

Christopher Columbus

Genoa's most famous son, Christopher Columbus, was born in the city in about 1451. His father, a weaver, is said to have lived in the small gatehouse near Porta Soprana, rebuilt in the 18th century, and tradition has it that Columbus was born here, but virtually nothing is known of his early life. When it came to his plan to sail west across the Atlantic to Asia, it was the newly united Spain rather than Genoa's Banco di San Giorgio that gave him financial backing. By reaching America (or, as he thought, Asia) in 1492, Columbus altered the whole pattern of world trade, stagnating expansion for the Mediterranean and his native city. Columbus died in 1506 still believing that he had reached Asia.

In 1453, when Constantinople fell to the Ottoman Turks, Genoa lost her Black Sea and Levantine ports (with the exception of Chios) to the Turks. In the wake of this huge strategic reversal, Genoa drew on experience and resilience to find new markets and commodities, stepping up activities in Iberia and participating in new initiatives on the West African coast and in the Atlantic islands.

French and Spanish Intervention

The great struggle between France and Habsburg Spain for dominance in Italy effectively ended at the Battle of Pavia in 1525 when the French were expelled from the Duchy of Milan. Confirmed by treaties in 1529 (Barcelona) and 1559

Andrea Doria

Genoa's great admiral, statesman and adventurer, Andrea Doria (1466–1560), came from one of the city's most ancient and powerful families. He began his career as a *condottiere,* a mercenary commander in the Italian Wars, before equipping eight galleys at his own expense and successfully waging war on Turks and pirates for 12 years, returning to his city laden with booty. He then entered the services of Francis I of France as governor-general of the French galleys. After the French defeat at Pavia, he switched allegiance to Charles V, Spanish king and Holy Roman Emperor, but only on condition that Genoa was granted its freedom. The French were driven out and Doria was received in triumph in the city in 1528. Although he declined the dogeship, he instigated a new constitution, referred to as 'The Aristocratic Republic', which endured until 1797. Even in old age he remained an active politician, resisting Charles V's attempts to place a Spanish citadel at Genoa. Although a virtual dictator, Doria was a true patriot who, by strength and political manoeuvring, guaranteed freedoms for the city when most of Italy was suffering stagnation and oppression under Spanish viceroys.

(Cateau Cambresis), a century and a half of Habsburg domination began. Charles V, Holy Roman Emperor and king of Spain, looked on the republic of Genoa as a base for the control of the Tyrrhenian Sea. Complicit in this was one of the foremost naval leaders of his time, Andrea Doria *(see opposite)*.

Genoa's comparative freedom under the Spanish enabled her bankers, who had become specialists in monetary exchange, to manage

Andrea Doria

large sums for the Spanish Crown. They effectively controlled Spanish and Neapolitan trade, and by about 1570 the Genoese were the principal bankers of Catholic Europe. This period saw the rise of grand palaces in Genoa's Via Garibaldi and Via Balbi, built by local merchants, bankers and patrician families.

From the mid-17th century the fortunes of Genoa, along with much of Italy, were shaped by the European wars of succession. During this period, the city was largely excluded from the prosperous northern European and transatlantic economy. In 1684 the French bombarded Genoa in retaliation for its support of Spain in Sicily, and in 1746 the city was occupied by the Austrians. In 1768 Genoa lost her last Mediterranean colony to France, leading to a period of decadence and economic decline. In 1796 Napoleon's armies occupied the city, establishing a French-controlled Ligurian Republic. Shortly afterwards some 30,000 Genoese died of disease or starvation when the Austrians laid siege to the city, aided by the British fleet. The French were expelled in 1814 but the Treaty of Vienna ceded Liguria, now called the 'the Duchy of Genoa', to the kingdom of Piedmont–Sardinia, ruled by the House of Savoy.

From Unification to the Present

The *Risorgimento* (movement for Italian independence) manifested itself in the bitter discontent of both Republican and anti-Piedmontese groups. The great champion of Italian unity and independence, Guiseppe Mazzini, was born in Genoa in 1805. While a member of the Carbonari, a secret society dedicated to the overthrow of absolute rule in Italy, he participated in a planned uprising in Liguria and was imprisoned in Savona. Garibaldi's great military campaign to free Sicily and southern Italy from the Bourbon monarchy began in Genoa, from where he sailed to Sicily in 1860, accompanied by his famous 'one thousand' red-shirted army. A year later Liguria became part of the new kingdom of Italy.

Peace brought the first waves of tourists at the end of the 19th century, when many fine villas along the rivieras were built. During World War II, Genoa was badly bombed, but after 1945 it regained its role as Italy's main seaport and saw a huge building boom and expansion of industries.

Remnant of the past: a fortified tower at Alassio

The rivieras were gradually developed for mass tourism, bringing in further prosperity. More recently the Porto Antico has been innovatively rebuilt by the Genoan architect, Renzo Piano *(see page 30)*, giving new life to the old port in time for the city becoming European Capital of Culture in 2004.

Historical Landmarks

80,000–30,000BC Neanderthal man and the later *Homo sapiens sapiens* inhabit Balzi Rossi caves.

205BC Genoa, allied to Rome, is destroyed by Carthage.

177BC Romans start to establish bases in Liguria.

568 Lombards invade Liguria.

774 Charlemagne, king of the Franks, brings Lombard rule to an end.

935 Genoa sacked by Saracen raiders.

1097 Genoa provides ships for First Crusade.

11th–12th century Genoa acquires trading colonies and sets the stage to become a dominant Mediterranean power.

12th century Communes are set up at Porto Maurizio, Savona, Albenga, Sarzana and Noli.

1284 Genoa defeats Pisa at Battle of Meloria.

1339 Simone Boccanegra becomes first doge of Genoa.

1380 Genoa defeated by Venice at the Battle of Chioggia.

1407 Founding of the Banco di San Giorgio.

1451 Christopher Columbus born in Genoa.

16th century Genoese become principal bankers of Catholic Europe.

1684 Genoa bombarded by the French.

1746 Austrians occupy Genoa but are later forced out.

1796 Short-lived Ligurian Republic created by Napoleon.

1814–15 Genoa ceded to the kingdom of Piedmont–Sardinia.

1805 Giuseppe Mazzini born in Genoa.

1860 Garibaldi sets sail from Genoa to free Sicily and southern Italy.

1861 Liguria becomes part of the proclaimed unified Italy.

1915 Italy enters World War I.

1940–45 Genoa suffers major bombing in World War II.

1984–92 Redevelopment of Genoa's old port.

1992 500th anniversary of Columbus' discovery of America.

1999 Cinque Terre National Park created.

2001 G8 summit held in Genoa.

2004 Genoa is European Capital of Culture.

WHERE TO GO

GETTING AROUND

Liguria is one the smallest regions of Italy, and you could cover most of the coast in a couple of weeks. The Via Aurelia (or SS1) hugs the coast for most of the way, linking coastal towns and villages. The *autostrada* is a quicker way of covering long distances, particularly in summer when coastal towns are choked with traffic. The highway winds tortuously and spectacularly above the coast, dipping down into dimly lit tunnels and swooping over huge viaducts. By car you can quickly reach the hills and valleys of the Maritime Alps and Apennines; but if you are not exploring inland, consider using public transport. The train service along the coast is excellent and in season the resorts east of Genoa are also accessible by ferry.

Sightseeing in Genoa could occupy two or three days, although you can get a good idea of the historic centre on a day trip to the city. Public transport within Genoa is good, but it's only by walking that you enter into the spirit of the city.

GENOA

The Old City

Genoa's medieval centre is built on a slope and crossed by a dense warren of narrow alleyways known as *carrugi*. Lofty dwellings make the streets feel dark even on the brightest days and some alleys are so narrow that a couple of Vespas can hardly squeeze by. For each laundry-draped tenement block there's a splendid ancient monument or a treasure-filled palazzo. The quarter is densely atmospheric,

Alleyway in the Old City

Rooftop view of the city

its streets teeming with tiny shops, from artisans and basic groceries to branches of Hermes and Louis Vuitton.

The city originated at Castello Hill, where Ligurian coastal traders settled in the 6th century BC. A Roman castle once stood here and the Church of Santa Maria di Castello, the oldest in the city, incorporates Roman columns and foundations. Dwellings in this quarter date back to the 12th century, and include the 41-m (134-ft) high **Embriaci Tower**, one of the loftiest of the many privately owned medieval towers which punctuated the skyline in medieval times. To the east, the **Church of San Donato** has a beautiful octagonal campanile and Romanesque interior. Also here is the Gothic (now deconsecrated) Sant'Agostino, whose monastery, destroyed in World War II, is now the **Museo di Sant'Agostino** (Piazza Sarzano; open Tues–Fri 9am–7pm, Sat–Sun 10am–7pm; admission fee; <www.museosantagostino.it>). The cloisters here provide the setting for architectural fragments, columns and sculptures salvaged from destroyed churches.

Medieval walls were constructed around the city in the mid-12th century. The only section that remains is the much-restored **Porta Soprana**, the gateway from the east. Just below it, the lovely **Sant'Andrea Cloister**, surrounded by olive trees and restored in 1992, is all that remains of the 12th-century monastery. Nearby, the little creeper-clad **Casa di Cristoforo Colombo** (open Sat and Sun 9am–noon, 3–6pm; admission fee) is reputedly the house of Domenico Colombo, father of Christopher Columbus. Tradition has it that the great navigator, born around 1451, spent his childhood here. Rebuilt in the 18th century, the house contains an unremarkable display of Columbus memorabilia.

Palazzo Ducale

Via di Porta Soprana brings you to Piazza Matteoti, dominated by the monumental neoclassical façade of the **Palazzo Ducale** (open Tues–Sun 9am–9pm; admission fee for exhibitions; <www.palazzoducale.genova.it>). It was given the name 'Palazzo Ducale' in 1339 when it became the seat of the first Genoese doge. In the 16th century the medieval structure was replaced by a new baroque palace, created to reflect the glory of the republic. Abandoned after

Viewpoints

The setting of the city, on a steep hill, lends itself to lifts and funiculars. Several were installed in the late 19th century and are still a popular means of transport. They are also a cheap and fast means of getting great views of the city. For the finest panorama take the funicular from Largo della Zecca that climbs 1430m (4690ft) to the hillside quarter of Righi.

Dome detail inside the Gesù

bombing in World War II, the palace has been restored to its former glory and is now a hub of the city's cultural and commercial activities. There are restaurants, cafés and bookshops, and the colonnaded courtyard and richly decorated council halls and chapel make splendid settings for temporary exhibitions. On the same square, Sant'Ambrogio, known as the **Church of the Gesù**, has a sumptuous baroque interior and two masterpieces by Rubens: *The Circumcision* over the high altar and *The Miracle of St Ignatius,* in the third chapel on the left.

Cattedrale di San Lorenzo

The dazzling black and white striped façade of the city's **Cathedral** (open daily 8am–noon, 3–7pm; free) makes a dramatic impact as you enter its piazza. Founded in 1118 when it replaced San Siro outside the city's walls as the cathedral, San Lorenzo was given a Gothic façade in the early 14th century. The dark and somewhat gloomy interior is enlivened by some richly decorated chapels. The loveliest of these is the **Chapel of St John the Baptist** on the left side, adorned with exquisite Renaissance reliefs by Andrea Sansovino and other leading sculptors. The chapel was created to protect the saint's ashes, which supposedly lie within the 13th-century urn. The underground **Museo del Tesoro** (open Mon–Sat 9am–noon, 3–6pm; admission fee) is a repository of precious relics including the Sacro Catino, a green glass bowl, brought back to Genoa in the 12th century as war booty, traditionally believed to have been the one that Jesus drank from at the Last Supper. Also here is the elaborate mid-15th-century processional casket for the ashes of St John the Baptist, which is carried through the streets of the city on 24 June each year.

Piazza San Matteo to Palazzo Spinola

Black and white marble bands are also the distinctive feature of nearby **Piazza San Matteo**. This beautifully preserved little square was the private seat of the powerful Doria family.

It was from here that Andrea Doria *(see page 18)* rallied the Genoese troops to revolt against the French in 1528. The family built the palaces flanking the square and the charming Church of San Matteo. The church façade is typically Gothic, but the interior was given a Renaissance makeover and elaborately decorated with frescoes, gilt and marble. Andrea Doria's sarcophagus lies in the crypt (ask the sacristan for access).

San Lorenzo cathedral

Streets to the west, such as Via Orefici (Street of the Goldsmiths), Vico degli Scudai (of the Coinmakers) and Vico degli Indoratori (of the Gilders), were the domain of merchants and bankers and you can still find goldsmiths here. **Piazza Bianchi** was the seat of the first money exchange, *bianchi* being the counters of the moneychangers and bankers in medieval times. The Loggia dei Mercanti (1595) was the hall of moneylenders and hosted the first stock exchange in 1855. Leading north, Via San Luca leads to the **Galleria Nazionale di Palazzo Spinola** (Piazza Superiore di Pellicceria 1; open Tues–Sat 8.30am–7.30pm, Sun 1.30–7.30pm; <www.palazzospinola.it>; admission fee). The palace was built by the Grimaldi family and later occupied by their rivals, the Spinolas. The lavish décor and the frescoed Gallery of Mirrors give you some idea of

Neptune, the movie-star galleon

their lifestyle. The Galleria Nazionale, housed here since the 1950s, features Italian and Flemish Renaissance works of art, including Antonello da Messina's *Ecce Homo* and works by Rubens and Van Dyck.

Porto Antico and the Waterfront

The Porto Antico (old port; <www.portoantico.it>), redeveloped under architect Renzo Piano *(see page 30)* between 1984 and 1992, is the tourist hub of the city. For an overview of both port and city, go to the Aquarium quayside and take a **boat tour**, which also allows you a glimpse of the galleon *Neptune*, built for Roman Polanski's movie, *Pirates*. Tours leave regularly, and last 45 minutes (€6 per person). From April to September a daily service operates to San Fruttuoso Bay and Portofino.

Turtle in the Aquarium

The number-one attraction in the port is the **Aquarium** (open Mon, Tues, Wed and Fri 9.30am–7.30pm, Thur 9.30am–10pm, Sat, Sun and hols 9.30am–10.30pm; last admission 1½hrs before closing time; admission fee; tickets available at <www.acquariodigenova.it>). This is the second most visited site in Italy – or that's what it claims – so be prepared for queues. Once inside, allow at least two hours to take in the huge diversity of marine life. There are over 6,000 species, from sharks, seals and bottlenose dolphins, through long-snouted wrasse and wide-eyed flounders to Nile crocodiles and tomato frogs. The Grande Nave Blu (Big Blue Ship) takes you on a journey of the great discoverers, and through the tropical habitats of Madagascar with their staggering diversity of species. Off the Aquarium pier, the futuristic glass bubble over the water is the **Biosfera**, a steamy habitat of tropical plants and butterflies.

Dominating the waterfront you can't miss **Il Bigo** or crane, the curious structure with white metallic arms, symbolic of ships' masts. The structure rises high above the port and a rotating panoramic lift hoists you up for a bird's-eye view of the city and waterfront. The awnings of the neighbouring Piazza delle Feste shelter an ice-skating rink in winter and a concert and theatre venue in season. The **Museo**

Nazionale dell'Antartide (National Antarctic Museum, Palazzina Millo; open summer Tues–Sun 10.30am–6.30pm, winter Tues–Fri 9.45am–5.30pm, Sat and Sun 10am–6pm; admission fee) is devoted to the South Pole and the research carried out there by the Italians.

The latest attraction is the **Galata Museo del Mare** (Galata Museum of the Sea; open Mar–Oct daily 10am–7.30pm;, Nov–Feb Tues–Fri 10am–6pm, Sat, Sun and hols 10am–7.30pm; admission fee), a four-storey glass structure on the Darsena waterfront north of the aquarium. The largest maritime museum of the Mediterranean, equipped with the latest technology, it charts the seafaring history of the city and port since medieval times.

If all this is not sufficient to keep the family occupied you could take them to **La Città dei Bambini** (Kids' City), a large educational and entertainment centre for children aged 3 to 14, located in an old cotton warehouse.

Rising on a solitary rock to the southwest, the lofty **Lanterna** (lighthouse) has been welcoming vessels for centuries.

Renzo Piano

It was apt that the architect who transformed the old port area of the city was the Genoese-born Renzo Piano. One of the world's leading contemporary architects, he has an impressive portfolio, ranging from the revolutionary Pompidou Centre in Paris (co-designed with Richard Rogers) in 1971 to the vast Kansai International Airport terminal on an artificial island in Japan's Osaka Bay (1994). No two buildings are alike but clear themes run through his work, typically an abundant use of natural light and a combination of cutting-edge technology and native building traditions and materials. The Porto Antico attractions all focus on the water and have marine themes. The most striking is Il Bigo which became a symbol of Expo 1992.

The tower stands 117m (383ft) above sea level and throws a beam for over 50km (30 miles). According to un-official documents, the first lighthouse on the site was built in 1128, when fires of heather and gorse were lit at the top of the tower to as-sist navigators. The Lanterna assumed its present form in 1543, and has become the historic symbol of Genoa.

Renzo Piano's Il Bigo

Sottoripa and Environs

Inland from the Porto Ant-ico, the medieval arches of Via di Sottoripa shelter small shops and stalls, hole-in-the-wall cafés and tiny deli-catessens doubling as bars. The sea used to come right up here – the cafés and restaurants enjoying pleasant port views – but nowadays these are blocked by waterside development and the brutal-looking *sopraelevata* (flyover). This 1960s eyesore, sitting on steel pylons, extends some 4km (2½ miles) and carries a noisy and seemingly endless flow of traffic. Plans to divert traffic under the harbour, reuniting the city with the sea, are still at the drawing-board stage and may remain that way.

The huge palace dominating the southern end of Via di Sot-toripa is **Palazzo Giorgio**. This has served variously as the seat of government, customs house and headquarters of the famous Banco di San Giorgio *(see page 17)*. Tradition has it that Marco Polo, who was held prisoner of war here in 1298, compiled an account of his travels with the co-operation of a fellow prison inmate, Rustichello of Pisa. The tales were later to become Polo's book *Il Milione* (his nickname was Marco 'Il Milione', of the million lies). The palace's waterfront façade with the fancy clock tower is gaudily frescoed with scenes replicating those on the original baroque palace, including a central depiction of St George and the dragon. Look closely and you'll see that all those niches and rustication on the palace are *trompes l'oeil*. In contrast, the north and east sides retain their medieval aspect, with Gothic arcades and brickwork, albeit rebuilt in the early 20th century.

The Baroque City: Via Garibaldi and Via Balbi

In 1551 Doge Grimaldi Bracelli opened a new street called the Strada Nuova (New Street), the present-day **Via Garibaldi**. A symbol of the wealth and power of the Genoese nobility, the street boasts a succession of monumental baroque palaces. Now restored to their original grandeur, the mansions make handsome settings for art galleries, prestigious banks or interior designers. The pedestrianised street is pleasant to stroll along and there is nothing to stop you wandering into elegant inner courtyards, admiring the frescoed ceiling of a bank or the chandeliers gleaming from the *piano nobile*.

Via Garibaldi

You can visit the interiors of Via Garibaldi's three main palaces, Rosso (No. 18), Bianco (No. 11) and Tursi (No. 9), with a combined ticket, available from the bookshop at Via Garibaldi 9. All three are open Tues–Fri 9am–7pm, Sat and Sun 10am–7pm.

Palazzo Rosso, named after the red-stone facing, houses a gallery of 15th- to 18th-century paintings,

Venere e Marte by Peter Paul Rubens in the Palazzo Bianco

featuring works by the likes of Veronese, Guercinon and Dürer. The second floor is enlivened with 17th-century ceiling frescoes depicting *Allegories of the Four Seasons* by the Genoese artists De Ferrari and Piola. Members of the Brignole-Sale family who built the palace are portrayed by Van Dyck, and there's a charming genre scene, *The Cook*, by Bernardo Strozzi (1581–1644), the leading Genoese painter of his period.

Across the road, **Palazzo Bianco** houses the finest of the city's art galleries. The collection starts with Filippino Lippi's *San Sebastian between St John the Baptist and Francesco* and moves on to a large collection of Flemish and Dutch masters, many of whom lived in Genoa working for patrician families. Notable works are *Christ Blessing* by Hans Memling, *Christ of the Coin* by Van Dyck, and works by Dürer and Rubens. The Spanish 17th-century school is represented by Murillo and Zubarán; the collection ends with 17th- and 18th-century works by Genoese artists.

The massive **Palazzo Tursi** next door was commissioned in 1564 by Nicolò Grimaldi, banker to Philip II of Spain, and today is the town hall. Rooms have been restored to house works of art, but the palace is best known as the repository of three letters of Christopher Columbus (not normally on view to the public) and two violins which belonged to Paganini. The 'Cannone', Paganini's favourite, bequeathed to the city in his will, is brought out once a year and played by the winner of the Premio Paganini, an international violin contest.

Palazzo Lomellino (also called Palazzo Podestà) at No. 7 stands out for the stucco and reliefs on the façade. The owner, Lomellino, built the palace on the proceeds of lucra-

Palazzo Spinola frescoes

tive coral-fishing activities on the Tunisian island of Tabarca. The richly decorated atrium leads into a courtyard which is closed by a grotto framed by two large tritons. If the doors of the neighbouring **Palazzo Spinola** (Deutsche Bank, No. 5) are open, have a peep at the ground-floor frescoes.

West of Via Garibaldi, **Via Balbi** was named after the enormously wealthy family of merchants who built the entire street in 1602–20. This too boasts some imposing baroque palaces but the relentless traffic and the grime that encrusts many of the buildings doesn't lend the street to relaxing sightseeing.

The restored Palazzo dell' Università in the baroque former College of the Jesuits at No. 5 has a fine inner courtyard. But the main tourist attraction is **Palazzo Reale** (No. 10; open Tues and Wed 9am–1.30pm, Thur–Sun 9am–7pm), the Royal Palace and home to the National Gallery. Originally a Balbi residence it was transformed into a royal residence for the House of Savoy and is richly decorated with frescoed and stuccoed

Paganini's violin in Palazzo Tursi

ceilings, antiques and paintings. Most lavish of all is the Galleria degli Specchi (Hall of Mirrors), embellished by allegorical ceiling frescoes and marble sculptures.

At the end of Via Balbi, an ingenious funicular-cum-lift whisks you up to the hilltop crowned by the **Castello D'Albertis** (open Tues–Sun, Apr–Sep 10am–6pm, Oct–Mar 10am–5pm; admission fee). The neo-Gothic castle has been completely restored and is now the setting for the stylish Museo delle Culture del Mondo, and the large collection of archaelogical and marine artefacts amassed by its owner, D'Albertis, and his cousin during their travels abroad. It is worth the trip for the views alone.

Palazzo del Principe (Doria Pamphili)

The monumental **Prince's Palace** (Via Adua 6; open Tues–Sun 10am–5pm; admission fee) was built in 1529–33 by the admiral and statesman Andrea Doria *(see page 18),* and is still in the hands of the Doria Pamphili princes. The views from the

By the fountain on Piazza de Ferrari

gardens and terraces sloping down to the sea changed radically when the city walls and a public road was constructed in the 1630s, and today it has a sad setting amid road junctions and railway lines. The most desirable and approriate arrival is by sea which you can do in summer on a reconstructed 16th-century frigate from the Porto Antico (departures every half hour 10am–1pm, 2.30–4pm). A leading patron of the arts, Andrea Doria commissioned Perin del Vaga, a pupil of Raphael, to enrich his palace with stunning frescoes and stuccoed ceilings. Andrea Doria's heir, Giovanni Andrea I, extended the palace with the Room of Paris, a family chapel and the stunning Golden Gallery which is hung with exquisite tapestries depicting the Battle of Lepanto (1571). The palace is in need of further restoration, but the elaborate decoration, furniture and paintings give you a good idea of the original splendour. (Audio guides, included in the ticket price, are useful since there is scant information in the rooms.)

Modern Genoa

A new hub of cultural and economic life was created by the spread of the city during the 19th and early 20th centuries. The heart of modern Genoa is **Piazza de Ferrari**, overlooked by neoclassical façades, enlivened by a large circular fountain but spoilt by the constant flow of traffic. The eastern façade of the Palazzo Ducale (*see page 25*) stands out for its pink and ochre *trompe l'oeil* columns and rustication. The **Teatro Carlo Felice** (Carlo Felice Theatre), fronted by a Doric colonnade, was rebuilt in 1987–91 following a 40-year closure after damage in World War II. A modern square tower was created, incorporating four state-of-the-art stages enabling rapid changes of scenes. Via XXV Aprile and Via Roma to the north of the theatre are lined by elegant shops, and the wide Via XX Settembre to the east has been the city's main shopping throughfare since the end of the 19th century. The arcaded boulevard is home to department stores, clothes shops and the Mercato Orientale, the covered food market. Cafés, bars and restaurants in the glassed-roofed Galleria Manzini behind the theatre make a welcome respite from the traffic-choked streets. Via Dante, off Piazza de Ferrari, brings you into the 20th century, with two skyscrapers (1935–41), which were considered highly innovative for their day.

Excursions from Genoa

An hour's train trip to the rural hill village of **Casella** provides a complete antidote to the frenzy of the city centre. You travel on the little narrow-gauge railway through unspoilt forested hills and valleys (for timetable and other information, visit <www.ferroviagenovacasella.it>). The train departs from Piazza Manin, a 20-minute bus ride from Stazione Brignole or Stazione Principe. Mountain bikes can be hired at the station and taken on the train.

The **Staglieno Cemetery** (Piazzale Resasco; open daily 7.30am–4.30pm) northeast of the centre is a fascinating outdoor gallery of 19th- and 20th-century sculpture. The cemetery spreads over 160 hectares (395 acres) and you could easily spend half a day exploring the elaborate monuments, statues and chapels. To get there take a taxi or No. 12 or 14 bus from Stazione Brignole. A bus service operates within the cemetery.

Genoa's 17th-century walls, extending over the hilltops, incorporate well-preserved **fortresses**, built by the Savoyards. These are best explored by driving along the scenic **Strada delle Mura** (Wall Road) which starts at Piazza Manin, north of the city centre.

Villas and Parks

Either side of Genoa, formerly fashionable seaside retreats favoured by northern European nobility, have been largely swallowed up by city suburbs. The main attractions are the surviving 18th- and 19th-century villas and their parks. West of the city, **Pegli** is home to the Villa Durazzo Pallavacini, which has an archaeological museum and sumptuous English-style park; and to the Villa Doria-Centurione housing a naval museum. Further along the coast,

City transport

quaint **Boccadasse** preserves its fishing-port character despite the development. **Nervi** is known for its parks, gardens and the lovely **Passeggiata Anita Garibaldi**, a 1.5-km (1-mile) long promenade along the seafront. Nervi's three villas, with museums and famous gardens, are now combined and known as the Nervi Parks.

Grand 19th-century seafront hotels in Bordighera

RIVIERA DI PONENTE

The Riviera di Ponente stretches some 150km (95 miles) from Ventimiglia on the French border to Genoa. At the end of the 19th century, wealthy British people came here for their winter holidays, attracted by the mild climate, garden villas and grand seafront hotels. The groomed sophstication disappeared long ago, and most of the coast is developed for modern tourism, but there are still charming medieval centres to explore, a beautiful hinterland and abundant lush gardens.

Ventimiglia

Travelling from the French border, **Ventimiglia** is the first main town of the Italian Riviera. (You also see it signed 'XXmiglia', but the name derives from the Intemelii Ligurian tribe and has nothing to do with '20 miles'.) In 1995 the town lost its *raison d'être* with the official removal of the borders, and later the

> **Beware of expensive bargains at Ventimiglia's market. A new decree against illegal street trading penalises the purchaser as well as the seller. At Ventimiglia, on-the-spot fines of €10,000 have already been imposed on individual foreigners buying fake designer goods such as Dior sunglasses or a Gucci handbag. The fine drops to a mere €3,333 if you pay within 60 days.**

introduction of the euro. Frontier traffic, which used to stop at Customs and then for coffee, souvenirs or exchange bureaux, now heads straight through. However, the French still flock across the border on Fridays for Ventimiglia's street market, the largest in Liguria (open 8am–4pm; come early and leave the car behind). Like the town, the market is not as chic as its French counterparts, but there are clothes and leather bargains, stalls with pesto sauce and pecorino cheese, and shops in the centre packed with bargain-rate cigarettes, wine and spirits.

Across the River Roia, the old quarter, **Ventimiglia Alta**, clings to a rocky spur and comprises a cluster of crumbling houses, steep, dark alleys and covered passageways. At its centre lies the Cattedrale dell'Assunta, a remodelled Romanesque church with a pretty baptistry at the back. The other Romanesque church is the over-restored San Michele near the town walls, overlooking the Roia valley.

Bearing witness to the more ancient town are the remains of the 5,000-seat **Roman amphitheatre** (3rd century BC), sadly sited between the main road and railway line, east of the modern town. Finds discovered here can be seen in the nearby Archaeology Museum at Forte dell'Annunziata (Via Verdi 41).

Among the many British travellers who were captivated by this stretch of coastline in the 19th century was Sir Thomas Hanbury, who had made his fortune importing tea and silk from the East. Spotting the glorious Cape Mortola from his yacht in the 1860s he decided to transform the myrtle-clad headland into a splendid park, filling it with plants imported from five continents. The site became the **Hanbury Gardens** (Capo Mortola, 5km/3 miles west of Ventimiglia; open daily mid-June–mid-Sept 9.30am–6pm, off-season 9.30am–5pm, winter 10am–4pm; admission fee). Owned by the Italian state since 1960, the gardens are gradually being restored to their former splendour. The parkland extends over 18 hectares (44½ acres), sloping down to the sea; half is covered by Mediterranean trees and scrub, the rest is planted with exotic flora such as succulents from the tropics, eucalyptus, citrus groves and some stunning climbers and roses. Allow at least two hours to follow the recommended paths.

Sir Thomas Hanbury also founded the **Museum of Pre-history** by the **Balzi Rossi caves** (open Tues–Sun 8.30am until 1hr before sunset; admission fee). A stone's throw from

Hanbury Gardens

the French border, at the foot of the cliffs, the museum displays ancient human and animal remains that were found in the nearby caves. The collection includes a 230,000-year-old human hip bone, skeletons of later Neanderthal man and *Homo sapiens sapiens*, tools, weapons, 'Venus' figurines, and jewellery made of shells. Waves permitting, you can visit two of the caves – which are no more than crevices in the Balzi Rossi (Red Cliffs).

Hilltop Villages

Ventimiglia is a good launching pad for excursions to the ancient **hilltop villages** of the mountainous interior. Hidden in the wooded Nervia valley or perched on mountaintops, the remote villages were built sufficiently far inland to escape the coastal raids of Saracen pirates in medieval times. Some are completely abandoned, others have been restored and are coming back to life. A tour of the villages along the mountain passes affords breathtaking views of the valleys and the coast below. It's also perfect country for hiking *(see page 84)*.

The following villages could easily be covered in a day trip from the coast. If time is limited, make sure at least to visit the medieval gem of **Dolceacqua** This is easily reached from Ventimiglia, either by bus, car or, for the ener-

Baiardo, a typical hilltop village

getic, a 10-km (6¼-mile) hike along the verdant Nervia Valley. The name means 'sweet water', though what this little town is famous for is the highly prized Rossese di Dolceacqua, a full-bodied, ruby-red wine, favoured by Napoleon who stayed here in 1796. The town straddles the River Nervia, which is spanned by the **Ponte Vecchio**, a picturesque 15th-century bridge. On the left bank lies the older 'Terra' quarter, in the shadow of the ruined **Doria Castle**. Proud and austere, this military fortress crowns a rocky pinnacle and dominates the entire town. Originally built by the counts of Ventimiglia, it was enlarged by the Doria family in the 12th to 14th centuries to become a noble residence.

Dolceacqua's old town is a fascinating labyrinth of narrow alleys and arched passageways, the ground floors of its tumbledown houses given over to craft workshops, galleries and little bars serving the local wine. The place is steeped in history, the most interesting snippets of which can be gleaned from the 'Tavolas' or information plaques around the town.

The feudal Dorias also occupied the castle at the ancient hilltop village of **Apricale**, reached by forking right at **Isolabona**. Here the cluster of grey houses tumbles dramatically down the hillside, high above the River Nervia. Commanding the surrounding countryside, the castle has been restored, its frescoed rooms now home to a small museum. It faces the beautiful main square, where plays and concerts are staged in summer. A spectacular and tortuous road snakes its way from Apricale to **Baiardo**. This medieval village clusters on a conical hill with glorious views of the Ligurian Alps from its terraces. At the top of the village the romantic ruins of the Church of San Nicolò bear witness to the earthquake of 1887 which devastated the town and killed over 200 of its inhabitants. The parish church, also dedicated to San Nicolò, was built lower down. You can return to the coast via **Ceriana**, another ancient village, which occupies a wooded peninsula high over the Armea Valley.

The square in Apricale

If you don't mind all the twists and turns, you can penetrate further into the Ligurian Alps and visit the fascinating little villages of **Pigna**, 9km (5½ miles) north of Isolabona and **Troira**, a further 29km (18 miles). Picturesquely perched on a hill, Pigna ('pine cone') may have acquired its name from the pine trees that once thrived here, or from its pine-cone shape, the houses creating concentric circles on the hill. The village has

Baiardo residents

fine valley views and notable works of art in its churches: San Michele has a stunning rose window and a huge polyptych of *San Michele* (1500) by Giovanni Canavesio, who also painted the frescoes of the *Passion of Christ* (1482) in the Church of San Bernardo in the cemetery.

The road snakes its way up to **Triora**, nicknamed 'Village of Witches' and precariously located on a mountain ridge in the upper Valle Argentina. Following a local famine in 1857, 200 women were put on trial for witchcraft and a dozen of them were burnt at the stake. You can find out more about it at the Ethnographical and Witchcraft Museum (open summer 3–6.30pm, winter 2.30–6pm, Sat and Sun 10.30am–noon, 2.30–6pm; admission fee). The theme is played out in the local shops selling sorceress dolls and a 'witches' liquor'. The village is also famous for snails and hosts a *sagra delle lumache* or snail festival in September. Sorcery and snails aside, Triora is an enchanting, semi-deserted village of narrow alleys, ancient houses and ruins of fortifications.

Bordighera

Since the inauguration of the Calais–Rome Grand Express in the 1870s, **Bordighera** has been welcoming travellers from cooler climes. From a little village and fishing port, the town became a fashionable resort, with palazzi and villas surrounded by parks and gardens. The place became a favourite holiday destination of writers, artists and royalty – Queen Margaret of Savoy stayed in a villa on the Via Romana for long periods and died here in 1926.

Nowadays the resort is popular with Italian families, though it is noticeably more peaceful than neighbouring San Remo. In winter it becomes a seaside retreat for the elderly. The town is famous for palm trees and has the exclusive right of supplying the Vatican with palm fronds in Holy Week. Lofty palms enhance the **Lungomare Argentina**, the long promenade which runs behind the string of pebble beaches. The development and main road behind the seafront are undistinguished, but just a little way inland the grandiose villas and hotels, set amid lush gardens, recall the resort's heyday. Among the town's British visitors was the remarkable Reverend Clarence Bicknell, a botanist and archaeologist who spent long hours studying the Bronze Age rock engravings of Monte Bego on the French–Italian border. Casts he made of the engravings can be seen at the **Museo Bicknell** (Via Bicknell; open Mon–Fri 9.30am–1pm, 1.40–4.45pm; free), founded by Bicknell in 1888. **Alta Bordighera**, the charming old town, stands inland above the coast, its quiet alleys, arcades and small squares protected within late medieval walls. This is a peaceful spot to come and dine, or to sample some of the local vintages in the *enotecas* (wine bars).

San Remo

In the centre of a wide sheltered bay **San Remo** (or Sanremo as the locals like to write it) is the *grande dame* of Ligurian res-

San Remo, *grande dame* of the Ligurian resorts

orts. This was the first resort to be established on the Italian Riviera and, like Bordighera, became a winter retreat for northern Europeans. Grand (or formerly grand) seafront hotels with names like 'Royal' and 'Grand Hotel & Des Anglais' are evidence of the town's glory days, and there are still wonderful Art Nouveau villas in the wooded hills behind the resort. The British were the first visitors. Then came Russian aristocrats who built large, elegant villas and founded **San Basilio**, the Russian Orthodox church with brightly coloured onion domes. The **Corso Imperatrice**, running along the seafront, was named after the Russian tsarina, Maria Alexandranova (wife of Tsar Alexander II), who lived here from 1874. A further reminder of those fashionable times is the Art Nouveau **casino** which, with its gaming rooms, roof garden, musical soirées and elegant restaurant, is still the focus of the town's social life.

San Remo is otherwise a large, modern resort with more hotels, facilities and entertainment than any other in Liguria.

San Remo flower market

While many of its residents are over 60, it is nevertheless a lively town – and with the staggering number of Vespas that screech through the centre, it can be quite a noisy one.

The garden-lined promenade skirts a string of beaches, from man-made sandy strips with the invariable lines of sunbeds to narrow pebble or rocky public beaches. For dining out, the most inviting quarter of San Remo is tree-shaded Piazza Bresco and Piazza Sardi, near the **Porto Vecchio** (old port) where fish are landed.

The old town of **La Pigna** perched on a hill could not be more of a contrast: a quaint cluster of crumbling houses and a maze of neglected alleys. Continue the steep climb and you come to the baroque sanctuary of Madonna della Costa with good views of the town and coast.

Alfred Nobel, the Swedish inventor of dynamite and founder of the eponymous prizes, lived in San Remo from 1891 until his death in 1896. It was thanks to one of his revolutionary inventions that he was banished from Paris and came to live in Italy. In 1887 Nobel invented ballistite, one of the first nitroglycerin smokeless powders. When the French turned down his offer of the patent (they had their own scientist working on a similar product) he turned to the Italians, who bought a large quantity of ballistite and purchased the patent. Incensed that a foreign national had experimented with military material in France and sold it to a member of the opposing Triple Alliance, the French unjustly charged Nobel with industrial espionage and threatened him with imprisonment. Suffering from ill-health, Nobel moved to the warm shores of the Mediterranean, bought a large seaside villa and had a laboratory built nearby. He did not endear himself to the neighbours when he built a jetty out to sea for testing gunpowder and firearms. Today the **Villa Nobel** in San Remo has a multimedia exhibition on the inventor's life and can be visited on guided tours (Corso Cavallotti 116; open July and Aug Sun and Wed 3pm, 4pm, 8pm, 10pm; Mar–June, Sep, Oct, Dec Sun only 3pm, 4pm; admission fee).

Bussana-Vecchia and Taggia

In the hinterland east of San Remo, the hill village of **Bussana-Vecchia** was devastated by the earthquake of 1887. A new village, Bussana, was built on the coast and the old one

Riviera dei Fiori

Since the 19th century, San Remo and its surrounds have been famous for a thriving industry in out-of-season cut flowers. Some 20,000 tonnes are annually exported or sold within Italy. The name Riviera dei Fiori (Riviera of Flowers) is nowadays somewhat misleading as most of the flowers are grown in glasshouses which can be seen glinting on the sunny slopes. As soon as the flowers are picked they are packed up in boxes and transported in refrigerated lorries to northern and central Italy or further afield up to northern Europe. Traditional exports include roses, carnations, mimosas and lilies, but competition from Third World countries such as Kenya, Colombia, Costa Rica, Ecuador and Morocco has led producers to focus on research into new varieties.

abandoned. Since the 1960s Bussana-Vecchia has been home to a colony of international painters and artisans who have restored some of the buildings. Galleries and craft shops line the steep cobbled streets, amid picturesque ruins sprouting wildflowers and weeds. The parish church at the top is an evocative, overgrown shell. Amazingly, virtually all the congregation on the day of the earthquake escaped unscathed.

West of San Remo, **Taggia** divides into two very different sections: Arma di Taggia, where sunseekers stretch out on the sandy beach, and Taggia, the medieval town inland, which gave its name to the black *taggiasca* olive. Apart from the impressive 16-arch medieval bridge over the River Argentina, the surroundings are not particularly inspiring; but once you are inside the town walls, this is a fascinating place to visit. Follow the yellow signs for the Itinerario Consigliato ('Recommended Route'), which takes you under arcades, along

Medieval inland town of Taggia

cobbled streets, and past crumbling palazzi, sculpted portals and black cavernous-looking interiors. Taggia too was hit by the 1887 earthquake and there is still major restoration to be done. The route takes you just outside the city walls to the **Convent Church of San Domenico** (open Mon–Sat 9am–noon, 3–5pm, until 6pm in summer; admission fee). The complex is a veritable museum of art. Within its 15th-century church are three fine paintings (above the high altar, and in the first and third chapels on the right) by Ludovico Brea (1443–c.1523), a painter from Nice. You can see the influence of Leonardo da Vinci, particularly in the landscape and the female face in the lovely *Madonna of the Rosary* (1513, first chapel on the right). The *Epiphany*, attributed to Parmigiani-no, was stolen several years ago but has been restored and returned to its place in the first chapel on the left. Other works of art include frescoes in the cloister, refectory and chapter house.

Imperia and Cervo

The provincial capital of **Imperia** was created in 1923 when Mussolini linked Porto Maurizio and Oneglia, either side of the River Impero. The two settlements had long been rivals: Porto Maurizio, formerly a free commune, was loyal to Genoa, while Ongelia was attached to Albenga, and after 1567 came under the control of the Savoys. You are not likely to linger long in either section, but of the two Porto Maurizio is the more interesting with its old **Parasio** quarter at the top of the hill. From the waterfront, it's a steep climb up, but a new cable car is currently under construction. Sadly much of the old town was pulled down by the Savoys to make way for the massive neoclassical cathedral; but there are still some medieval alleys to explore and a handful of Renaissance and later palaces, albeit in a dilapidated state. Borgo Marino down below is quite appealing with its waterfront quarter of boats, fish restaurants and a nearby beach.

Across the river at Via Gressio 13 is the main tourist attraction of Oneglia, the **Museo dell'Olivo** (Olive Tree Museum; open Mon–Sat 9am–noon, 3–6.30pm; <www.museo dellolivo.com>). This privately owned, award-winning museum traces the history of the olive tree from around 7,000 years ago. Eighteen sections cover every imaginable aspect of olive trees, olives and olive oil: cultivation, oil extraction, transport, trading and the various cosmetic and medicinal applications over the centuries. A shop on the premises sells the delicate Fratelli Carli olive oil and other oil-related products.

If you are heading east from Imperia, skip Diano Marina, the most solidly commercial resort of Liguria, and save your time for picturesque little **Cervo**, clinging to the steep hillside high above the coast. Its nickname is *Paradiso dei Pittori*, Painters' Paradise, and you will soon see why. Not only does it boast a beautifully preserved medieval centre, but it has the bonus of open sea-view terraces, a majestic baroque church rising over its rooftops and, at the very top, the ruins of a castle, now home to an ethnographical museum. The church, built chiefly with the funds from Cervo's coral fishermen, looks spectacular when floodlit at night and makes a stunning backdrop for the International Festival of Chamber Music in July and August.

The Widows' Reef

Laigueglia thrived on the coral trade in the 17th and 18th centuries, its fishermen travelling as far as Sardinia and Tunisia to find the coral colonies. The story goes that a coral reef was once spotted off the shores of Laigueglia. The local fishing fleet set sail to find it but a storm blew up off the coast and the boats capsized. None of the fishermen returned and the coral reef was never discovered.

Laigueglia, with its distinctive church towers, is little changed

Laigueglia and Alassio

Lying on the same huge sweep of bay as Alassio, **Laigueglia**
is heralded by the prominent twin towers of its baroque
church. It may not be as large or as glamorous as its more
famous neighbour, but it has a more peaceful atmosphere,
good soft-sand beaches, and a very appealing old quarter of
arcades, alleys and piazzas. Framed photos of Laigueglia in
the 1910s and 20s, posted around town, show that the town-
scape hasn't changed dramatically. A handful of fishermen
still land the daily catch at the pretty beach at the northern
end by the tower. One of three 16th-century fortifications,
the tower was built to defend the village from Saracen
attacks. Each summer, locals don pirate garb and re-enact
the invasions of that era.

From Laigueglia you can take a steep, winding road up to
Colla Micheri (3km/2 miles). This enchanting little hamlet
was restored in the 1960s and 70s by Thor Heyerdahl, the

Norwegian ethnologist and adventurer who led the 'Kon-Tiki' and 'Ra' expeditions. After his transoceanic adventures, he settled on this little cluster of rustic buildings as a second home.

From the village you can walk along the old mule path through the olive groves to the ruins of the Castle of Andora and the beautiful Romanesque/Gothic Church of Saints Giacomo and Filippo.

Known as 'the jewel of the Riviera', **Alassio** was one of the most elegant resorts in the early part of the last century. Northern Europeans were drawn by the luxurious hotels, sweeping sands, flowering gardens and hilltop villas. Today it is one of the Riviera's largest and most popular resorts, thanks largely to its fine, soft sands which stretch for nearly 4km (2½ miles). Not a lot survives from medieval times, but the town has a civilised centre with abundant

The fine sands of Alassio

cafés and fish restaurants, a
pleasant seafront prome-
nade, clubs and discos,
sports and cultural pursuits.
The resort caters for the
more affluent Italian families and foreigners – there
is virtually no public beach
and the entire sweep of the
bay is taken up by smart
concession areas and beach
clubs. A big bonus is the
easy access – you don't
have to cross the railway to

**Alassio's Muretto,
wall of fame**

get there. A few of Alassio's famous visitors have left their
mark on the **Muretto** (Little Wall) of Piazza Libertà. The
owner of the nearby Caffè Roma decided to put up ceramic
plaques with the autographs of celebrities who frequented
his bar. Among the first to receive the honour was Ernest
Hemingway, who stayed here in 1922. The signatures of
Winston Churchill, Sophia Loren and a host of other less
famous society figures, footballers and beauty queens can
also be found here.

Shopping in Alassio is a popular pastime, especially along
Via XX Settembre, the traffic-free alley running parallel to
the beach, more commonly known as the **Budello**. The construction of a vast new hotel with a multi-storeyed underground car park (for public as well as hotel use) is currently
disrupting the centre and will continue to do so until work
finishes in 2007. The hotel is being built on the site of the old
Grand Hotel of Alassio, the most desirable accommodation
in the resort until the 1960s. The beach right in front of it
was one of the locations for Alfred Hitchcock's first film,
The Pleasure Garden (1925).

All along the Riviera houses and palazzi have *trompe l'oeil* shutters, balconies, balustrades and columns – and they really do look real. The façades were painted either for reasons of economy (Ligurians have a reputation for thrift) or, more likely, the streets were too narrow to accommodate the sculptural details.

In summer, boats run regularly to the tiny island of **Gallinara**, a short way out to sea between Alassio and Albenga. The name derives from *galline* or wild hens, which, according to Roman scribes, lived here in ancient times. Today the herring gull dominates, nesting on the south-facing rocks. In medieval times the island was home to a powerful Benedictine monastery, but all that remains is the watchtower added in 1596. Today the island is privately owned and protected by a nature reserve.

Albenga

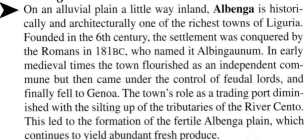

On an alluvial plain a little way inland, **Albenga** is historically and architecturally one of the richest towns of Liguria. Founded in the 6th century, the settlement was conquered by the Romans in 181BC, who named it Albingaunum. In early medieval times the town flourished as an independent commune but then came under the control of feudal lords, and finally fell to Genoa. The town's role as a trading port diminished with the silting up of the tributaries of the River Cento. This led to the formation of the fertile Albenga plain, which continues to yield abundant fresh produce.

Albenga nowadays is a large town, but the beautifully preserved ancient core is very compact and the pedestrian streets, following the Roman grid pattern, make for easy strolling. The hub is **Piazza San Michele**, where palaces and leaning towers cluster around the **Cattedrale di San Michele**. This Romanesque/Gothic cathedral was built over the original 5th-century Christian church. Just behind the cathedral don't miss the peaceful little **Piazza dei Leoni**, protected by three weather-beaten lions that came from Rome in 1607. Albenga's number-one architectural showpiece is the **Baptistry**, the oldest early Christian church in Liguria, dating from the first half of the 5th century. You reach it via the **Museo Civico Inguano** beside the cathedral in the Palazzo Vecchio del Comune (open Tues–Sun 10am–12.30pm, 2.30–6pm; admission fee). The museum comprises the Consuls' Room and the loggia, used for meetings of the Town Council, and today the setting for architectural finds from Roman, Byzantine and medieval Albenga. Steps lead down to the baptistry, showing you the level of the town in the 5th century. Within the polygonal structure (10 sides externally, 8 within) the eye is immediately drawn to the charming and rare Byzantine mosaic dating from around AD500, depicting the Trinity and the Apostles, represented by 12 doves. Note, too, the baptismal font and the late-medieval tombs with Lombard decorations.

Albenga Baptistry

Just across Piazza San Michele is the former Archbishop's Palace, Palazzo Peloso-Cepolla, which today houses the fascinating **Museo Navale Romano** (Roman Naval Museum; same opening hours as Museo Civico

Ingauno, above). The chief exhibits are the wine amphoras, salvaged in 1950 from the wreck of a large Roman cargo ship which sank off the coast here in the lst century BC. The ship contained over 10,000 jars of wine, hazelnuts and pickles.

The Varatella Valley north of Albenga is riddled with caves, the most famous among them being the **Grotte di Toirano** (open daily 9.30am–12.30pm, 2–5pm, until 5.30pm in summer; admission fee; guided tours). This extensive network of caves lies beyond the medieval hamlet of Toirano, 15km (9 miles) from Albenga. Foot- and handprints of Palaeolithic man were discovered in the Grotta della Bàsura (Witch's Grotto) along with the paw prints and bones of bears which can be seen in the Bear Cemetery. An artificial tunnel leads to the Grotta di Santa Lucia, which is embellished with staggering stalagmites and stalactities.

Finalborgo

On a splendid coast of craggy cliffs and wooded mountains, **Finale Ligure** stands out among a string of dull seaside resorts. The town comprises three different communities which were amalgamated in 1927. **Finale Marina** is a seaside resort with good beaches, a bustling seafront strung with open-air eateries, bars and discos and an appealing old town with arcades. **Finalpia** lies to the east, across the river and above the coast. The Church of Santa Maria di Pia, originally a medieval chapel, became the abbey church of the adjoining monastery in the 16th century and was given a pink rococo facelift two centuries later. The abbey is open to the public and you can buy honey and other products made by the monks.

Inland, **Finalborgo** is the most picturesque of the three, an enchanting walled city founded by the Del Carretto family in the 12th century, and rebuilt in the 15th century after destruction by the Genoese. The main entrance (Porta Reale or Royal

Gate) is heralded by the charming late-Gothic campanile of the **Church of San Biagio**. The plain grey church façade belies a majestic baroque interior, full of paintings, frescoes and sculpture. From here you can stroll through the unspoilt streets and squares, soaking up the atmosphere and stopping off at cafés or little osterias for regional dishes and local wines. Street signs will direct you to the **Convent of Santa Caterina**, now a cultural complex, where the late 15th-century cloisters make a fine setting for the **Archaeological Museum** (open Tues–Sun July–Aug 10am–noon, 4–7pm, Sept–June 9am–noon, 2.30–5pm; admission fee; <www.museoarcheo finale.it>). The collection ranges from the remains of Neand-herthal man through Roman funerary inscriptions to medieval ceramics and coins. Some of the later dated finds came from the ruins of Castel Gavone near the hamlet of Perti. The cas-tle's distinctive 'Diamond Tower' is visible from Finalborgo.

A quiet street in Finalborgo

Noli's ruined castle

Noli

Beyond the seaside village of Varigotti, with its multi-coloured fishermen's houses, the Via Aurelia skirts the headland before arriving at **Noli**, one of the best-preserved historic centres in Liguria. Referred to locally as 'The Fifth Maritime Republic' – the others being Genoa, Venice, Pisa and Amalfi – the town was a major seaport and, with the aid of Genoa, enjoyed six centuries of maritime prominence and political independence (1202–1797). Allied with Genoa from 1202, when it fought against Pisa and Venice, the town displays the influence of Genoese architecture in its dark narrow streets, porticoes and palaces. On the rugged Monte Ursino the ruined castle still keeps guard, its battlements marching down the hill to link with the old town walls. Noli once bristled with about 70 towers. Eight still stand, including the beautifully preserved 13th-century Torre Comunale in the centre, with Ghibelline crenellations. Finest of the churches is the glorious Romanesque **San Paragorio** on the west side of town, with its apse facing the sea. The exterior alone is worth a visit, but if the church happens to be open (summer Tues, Thur, Sat and Sun 10am–noon, winter Thur 10am–noon) you can see the Romanesque pulpit and crucifix, a medieval bishop's throne and 15th-century frescoes.

Noli's beach is one of the few along the coast where fishermen still land the daily catch. The boats are winched up the sands and the fish (red mullet and mackerel), squid and octopus are laid out in boxes on the palm-lined seafront and sold to the locals. For bathing you're better off at the beach of the large resort of **Sportorno**, just along the coast. D. H. Lawrence rented a villa here with his wife Frieda for several months in 1925. His stay here is reputed to have inspired his novel, *Lady Chatterley's Lover*. The peaceful little place in Lawrence's day is now a large modern resort and his villa was gutted in 2002 to make way for modern apartments.

Savona

Intimidating post-war industry and port activity dominate Savona, the provincial capital and largest town of the western Riviera. But the small old quarter near the harbour is worthy of a diversion and refreshingly untouristy. For some three centuries Savona enjoyed commune status, but a long and fierce rivalry with Genoa culminated in the destruction of the old town and port in 1528. The port was heavily bombed in World War II, but you can still see vestiges of the medieval

Savona's cruise-liner port

Street shrine in Savona

town and, from the Savoy era, piazzas and porticoes.

When the Genoese flattened the old town on the promontory, they replaced it in 1544 with the **Fortezza del Priamar** (Priamar Fortress; open Mon–Sat 7am–midnight, Sun and hols 10am–midnight; free). The imposing bulk (whose name dervies from *pietra sul mare,* 'stone over the sea') has served various functions over the centuries. Giuseppe Mazzini, revolutionary and leader in the Italian struggle for independence, was a prisoner here in 1830. Today the fort is a cultural complex housing an archaeological museum (open summer Tues–Sat 10am–12.30pm, 4–6pm, Sun 4–6pm, winter until 5pm; admission fee), the Museo Renata Cuneo (currently closed) with works by the Savona sculptor, and the Museo Sandro Pertini (open Sat and Sun 10am–noon; admission fee), a collection of modern art that belonged to Pertini, president of Italy from 1978 to 1985. The **Pinacoteca Civica** (open Mon–Sat 8.30am–12.30pm; admission fee), housing a large collection of paintings, sculpture and ceramics from medieval to modern times, has moved from the fort to the Palazzo Gavotti in the historic centre.

From the fort, you can walk down to the old port where pleasure craft and the occasional vast cruiser dwarf the few remaining boats of the fishing fleet. Three towers survive from medieval times, including the short Leon Pancaldo tower, the last remnant of the city walls, named after a Savonese sailor who accompanied Magellan on his travels in the early 16th century. From Piazza del Brandale, dominated by the heavily restored Brandale Tower, take **Via Pia**, the main street of the medieval city and home to some of the most important medieval and Renaissance palazzi.

Savona prides itself on the fact it produced two popes: Sixtus IV, who built the Sistine Chapel in the Vatican, and his nephew Julius II (a local fisherman in his early life) who commissioned Michelangelo to paint the chapel ceiling. Savona has its own **Cappella Sistina** (open Sat 10am–noon, 4–5.30pm; Sun 4–5.30pm; free guided tours on Sun), commissioned by Sixtus IV in 1471–84 as a funereal chapel for his parents. Don't expect a replica of its illustrious counterpart in the Vatican. A relatively simple chapel, it was given a complete stucco and gilt rococo transformation in 1715. The finely carved Renaissance tomb, showing the pope presenting his parents to the Madonna, has survived

Inside Savona's Cappella Sistina

from the original chapel. The highlight of the **Cattedrale di Santa Maria Assunta**, accessed via the cloister, is the early 16th-century choir, which was completely dismantled from the old cathedral and reassembled here to fit the shape of the semicircular apse. The choir seats are decorated with magnificent marquetry, depicting saints. To see the exquisite detail, ask the sacristan to switch on the lights.

Altare and Le Albisole

A detour of 15km (9 miles) west of Savona brings you to **Altare**, a town in the Apennines famous for glass production. Craftsmen from Normandy are believed to have brought the technique here in the 11th century and by the 15th century the town was second only to Murano in Venice for Italian glassware. Murano and Altare glass are almost indistinguishable, but whereas the Venetian craft was a

Lungomare degli Artisti, Albissola Marina

closely guarded secret, and glassmakers left the shores of Venice on penalty of death, Altare had no such restrictions. Local craftsmen were free to set up glassworks elsewhere in Europe and disseminate Venetian styles and techniques. Exquisite examples of locally produced glass can be seen at the Museo dell'Arte Vetraria Altarese (open Wed–Sun 3.30–7pm and Sat 10am–noon; admission fee), now housed in the Art Nouveau Villa Rosa, Piazza del Consolato.

While Altare is famed for glass, **Le Albisole** on the coast is synonomous with ceramics. Back in its heyday, in the 17th and 18th centuries, local craftsmen opened ceramic workshops all over Europe. Today both **Albissola Marina** (with a double 's'), the beach resort, and **Albisola Superiore** (with one 's') continue the production, with numerous studios and shops selling ceramics. Fine examples of 15th- to 20th-century local ceramics can be seen in the Museu Trucco (Corso Ferrari 193, Albisola Superiore; open Tues–Sat 10am–noon, Sun 3.30–6.30pm; free) and works by modern ceramicists can be viewed at the Fabbrica Museo 'Giuseppe Mazzotti 1903' (Via Matteotti 29, Albissola Marina; open daily 10am–noon, 4–6pm; free). The seafront promenade or *Lungomare degli Artisti* is paved in colourful mosaic ceramics created in 1963.

Sassello

The cool breezes of **Sassello**, up in the Apennines 23km (14 miles) north of Le Albisole, provide a welcome respite from the heat and hassle of the coast. A pretty 18th-century town, it is best known for the almond-flavoured *amaretti* biscuits. For information on local hiking, flora and fauna, visit the Visitors Centre for the Monte Beigua Regional Nature Park at Via G.B. Badano 45. The nature reserve extends for 18,160 hectares (44,870 acres) between Sassello and the coast, with Monte Beigua rising to 1,287m (4,222ft).

RIVIERA DI LEVANTE

Favoured by Shelley and Byron, the Levante is still the loveliest and most romantic of the two Rivieras. It can't boast good beaches (most are narrow stretches of pebble), but it has wild and spectacular cliff scenery and some enticing little ports and villages. Unless you're touring inland, a car can be more of a hindrance than a help. An excellent train service links the towns and villages, or in season you can go by sea, hopping on and off the ferries.

The Portofino Peninsula

Between the gulfs of Paradiso and Tigullio, the Portofino Peninsula is a coastal conservation area, the **Parco Naturale di Portofino**. Hiking trails offer glorious coastal views and a wealth of flora. Monte di Portofino, at 610m (2,000ft) is the highest peak. In the park's lower levels, cypress- and olive-studded slopes provide the backdrop for seductive little towns and resorts.

West of the headland, **Recco**, which was devastated in World War II, is no beauty spot but enjoys a reputation as the gastronomic capital of Liguria and is famed for its

Camogli's Fish Festival

Should you happen to be close to Camogli in early May and feeling peckish, head straight for Camogli's *Sagre del Pesce*. The fish festival celebrates San Fortunato who is said to have saved Camogli residents from drowning. On the night of the second Saturday of the month, large bonfires are lit and a huge green dragon and giant windmill are burnt on the seafront. The following day one and half tonnes of small fish are fried in a pan measuring nearly 4m (13ft) in diameter, and handed out to all and sundry.

focaccia al formaggio. However, most visitors prefer to head straight through and relax at the cafés and seafood eateries on the waterfront of nearby **Camogli**. The appealing little port shelters on the edge of the Portofino promontory, its lofty, pastel-washed houses wedged along the seafront. Go for a stroll along the promenade, stopping for coffee, *focaccia* or a seafood meal. You might also like to indulge in a spot of sunbathing on the steeply shelving pebble beach.

The 'saltiest, roughest, most piratical little place' as Charles Dickens described Camogli in 1884, is today one of the most popular excursion spots of the eastern Riviera.

Although tourism predominates, Camogli still has a fishing fleet whose boats bring in the catch every day at 5pm. The favourite annual event of the town is the fish festival *(Sagra del Pesce)* on the second Sunday in May when thousands of fish are fried up in a giant pan and distributed free on the quay *(see opposite)*.

At the western end of the beach, the much-altered medieval Dragon Castle (closed to the public) and the Basilica of Santa Maria Assunta occupy a rocky promontory, which was formerly an islet linked to the coast by bridge.

The name of the town may have come from *c'à a muggi*

('piled houses') or *cà a mogge* ('house of the wives'), the latter description dating back to the days when Camogli's seafarers departed on long voyages, leaving their wives behind. In the late 18th-century Camogli was a major port, supporting a fleet of 700 vessels. You can find out more about the town's maritime history in the Museo Marinaro (Maritime Museum, Via Ferrari 41; open Mon, Thur, Fri 9am–noon; Wed, Sat, Sun 9am-noon,3–6pm; admission fee).

From Camogli, you can take a ferry or the scenic footpath (three hours one way) to **San Fruttuoso**, a tiny rocky cove with a beautiful old Benedictine abbey (open June–Sept Tues–Sun 10am–6pm, March–May and Oct Tues–Sun 10am–4pm, winter hols only 10am–4pm, closed Nov; admission fee). The pale grey abbey, crowned by an octagonal tower, overlooks a little shingle beach and is dominated on the east side by the Doria Tower, built to ward off Turkish pirates. The church

The abbey and cove at San Fruttuoso

was built by the Benedictines in the 10th century and later renovated and extended by the powerful Doria family in exchange for the right to use the abbey as a family burial place. In the 1980s the abbey was bequeathed by the Dorias to the FAI (Italy's National Trust) who have since restored it. The lovely Romanesque cloister with sea views through Gothic lancet windows shelters the Doria tombs as well as a collection of ceramics and seals.

Ferry trips from San Fruttuoso

Because San Fruttuoso is accessible only by boat or foot, the tiny cove is packed in season. The inlet is also a favourite spot of scuba divers who swim down through limpid waters to the bronze statue of Cristo degli Abissi (Christ of the Depths). The statue was lowered to the seabed (17m/55ft down) in 1954 in honour of those who had lost their lives at sea.

Portofino

A 30-minute ferry trip or a 2½-hour hike over the clifftops and through vineyards and orchards, will take you from Camogli to the exclusive little port of **Portofino**. You can also go by car, but the beautiful corniche road from Santa Margherita Ligure is notoriously congested and parking prices are the highest in the Riviera (€19–22 a day – or take the bus for €1).

Remarkably, this tiny ex-fishing village, on a small, inaccessible inlet, became Italy's premier resort in the late 1950s and 60s, drawing the rich and famous and commanding some of the highest prices in Italy. It is remarkable too that, in spite of

Portofino, home to the Ligurian jet set

the huge number of day-trippers, it has managed to preserve its picture-postcard charm. The setting is idyllic, with quaint, multicoloured houses clustered around the harbour, steep green hills rising up behind and villas hidden amid olive groves. Strolling around the port, looking at the boats and houses, or people-watching at cafés are the main tourist pursuits; but you can also take a pleasant walk along the cliffs as far as the lighthouse at the end of the promontory (follow the 'Al Faro' signs from the port). The route goes via the **Church of San Giorgio**, containing what are said to be the remains of St George, whose feast day is celebrated on 23 April with festivities and a bonfire in the piazza. Further along, **Castello Brown** (open daily 10am–7pm; admission fee), built to command the Gulf of Tigullio, was occupied variously by the Genoese, English, Austrians, French and Savoys. The name originates from Montague Brown, an Englishman who bought it from the state in 1870 and converted it into a private residence. The English-style garden terraces afford glorious views of the gulf and resort; inside, framed black-and-white photos will remind you of the star-studded cast who fell for the charms of Portofino in the days of *La Dolce Vita*.

If you can afford to stay the night, the village is best seen when all the day-trippers have departed. The finest hotel is the

suitably named **Splendido** tucked away above the harbour and still exuding old-style glamour. The roll call of illustrious guests includes royalty and film stars. A double room with a sea view will set you back €1,330 a night *(see page 134)*.

Santa Margherita Ligure
Santa Margherita Ligure (or 'Santa' as it's known) may not be quite as chic as Portofino, but it's certainly one of the most fashionable and lively resorts of Liguria. The setting on the lovely Gulf of Tigullio has attracted travellers since the 19th century when it became a winter watering hole for wealthy British. It still retains a handful of hotels with an Edwardian, if

Feeding time, Santa Margherita

faded grandeur and some glorious villas hidden in the green, hilly hinterland. The resort makes a great base, with an excellent rail service to the Cinque Terre, dozens of ferries in season and plenty of waterfront restaurants and bars. Life focuses on the palm-lined promenade and the harbour with its luxury yachts. There are streets of elegant shops and a *pescheria* (fish market) on the edge of the harbour where you can join the crowds waiting to see what the local fishing fleet brings in. Above the town, the Villa Durazzo in a park of lofty palms, was a favourite residence of prominent 19th-century visitors. Today the elegant rooms are the setting for concerts, congresses and cultural activities. Santa's beaches aren't particularly alluring, but you can swim from rocks or platforms or take a bus to Paraggi beach to the south.

Rapallo

Long before it was developed for tourism, **Rapallo** became a favourite haunt of poets and writers, drawn by the beauty of the bay and the steep wooded mountains of the hinterland. Today it's a large resort, lacking the cachet of Portofino and Santa Margherita Ligure but offering abundant facilities and events. The palm-lined promenade ends picturesquely with the 16th-century castle, built in response to a bloodthirsty attack by the Turkish fleet. The castle has been restored and is today used as an exhibition centre. On the eastern edge of town the Villa Tigullio in the Parco Casale houses some exquisite examples of lacework in its **Museo del Merletto** (Lace Museum). Not to be missed is the cable car, which climbs 2,349m (7,707ft) to the **Santuario di Montallegro** behind Rapallo, with stunning ◀ views over the valley and bay (open summer daily 7am–noon, 2.30–7pm, winter daily 8am–noon, 2.30–5pm; cable cars depart every 30 mins and take 7 mins). This 16th-century pilgrimage church was built to protect a Byzantine icon of the Madonna that miraculously appeared here in 1557. A three-day festival in July celebrates the Madonna.

Chiavari to Sestri Levante

The Via Aurelia corkscrews along the coast to Zoagli, renowned for the production of silk and damask *(see page 92)*.

Chiavari

Further on, **Chiavari** is a large town and resort with a flat, unremarkable coastline but an appealing historic centre. The hub of the town is picturesque Piazza Mazzini, filled every morning by a lively fruit and vegetable market and overlooked by the huge neo-Gothic Palazzo di Giustizia (Palace of Justice). The surrounding medieval arcades shelter shops selling antiques, macramé and the traditional balloon-backed wood and straw campanina chairs – as well as fashion boutiques.

Inspired by the beautiful promontory setting of **Sestri Levante** when he stayed here in 1833, the writer

Hans Christian Andersen named the main bay the **Baia delle Favole** (Bay of Fables). Today the bay is the main focus of tourism, with palm trees and gardens enhancing the seafront. On the other side of the isthmus, the **Baia di Silenzio** may not quite live up to its name, but it's the more peaceful of the two, with a lovely sheltered crescent of fine sand overlooked by pastel-washed houses. The road up to the wooded headland takes you past the ruins of the **Oratory of Santa Caterina**, destroyed in World War II, and beyond it the lovely little 12th-century church (restored in the 17th century) of **San Nicolò dell' Isola** (closed to the public). The magnificently sited Grand Hotel dei Castello was converted from three castles built here in the 1920s by a lawyer who bought the whole peninsula and lived here with his retinue of servants. The private park features a tower from which Marconi carried out some of his first high-frequency radio experiments.

> **In July 1934, Guglielmo Marconi conducted a blind navigation experiment using the yacht *Elettra*. Equipped with a VHF radio system, *Elettra* sailed from Santa Margherita to the small port of Sestri Levante, guided solely by signals received by the transmitter on top of a 12th-century Genoese lookout tower – today's Marconi Tower.**

The Cinque Terre

Teetering on the rugged and precipitous cliffs northwest of La Spezia are the five ancient former fishing villages known as the **Cinque Terre**. At one time remote communities, only accessible by boat, they now make up one of northern Italy's most-visited attractions. From May to October boatloads and trainloads of travellers descend on the little ports and railway stations, crowding out the narrow streets and squares; and the centuries-old footpaths linking the villages are now trodden

Corniglia, least visited of the Cinque Terre villages

by hundreds of hikers every year. To avoid the crush, come in early spring or winter, or stay the night in a local B&B so you can at least see the villages before the mid-morning onslaught, and at sunset when peace descends again.

To protect the area, the Cinque Terre was declared a World Heritage Site in 1998 and the area has been designated a national park. Cinque Terre cards *(see page 76)* control the tourist flow, and must now be purchased by anyone using the cliff (or other) paths. There are strict controls regarding development and, despite commercialism, the villages are still the stuff of picture postcards. Each has a Gothic church and, typically, a cluster of pastel-coloured houses clinging to the rocky slopes, around a central piazza.

Remarkably, 11,000km (nearly 7,000 miles) of dry-stone walls were created over the centuries on the seemingly vertical cliffs for the cultivation of vines. Murals at Riomaggiore near the station demonstrate the backbreaking work of digging the soil and building the walls. The wines produced in the region are the fragrant and fruity white Cinque Terre and the rarer Sciacchetrà dessert wine made from grapes which are left to dry on racks all summer.

All five villages are accessible by road, but cars are very much discouraged. The drive down on tortuous, narrow roads is arduous and time-consuming, with queues in summer to get

---

Getting Around the Cinque Terre

The best way to appreciate the Cinque Terre scenery is to walk from village to village along the cliff path. Some stretches are strenuous but it's worth the effort for the breathtaking views. The entire walk, known as the **Sentiero Azzurro** (Blue Trail) is 12km (7½ miles) long, takes five hours and is at its most arduous from Corniglia to Monterosso. At the end of the hike you can take the train back to your starting point – or hop on it at any station if you run out of steam. If you want a more peaceful path, try the **Strada dei Santuari**, which connects the five sanctuaries above the villages. Hikers in good shape could also consider the **Sentiero Rosso** (Red Trail), a 23-km (14½-mile) path that runs along the ridgetop between Levanto and Portovenere, southeast of Riomaggiore. The walk takes 9 to 10 hours.

Information offices in all villages supply maps of the footpaths and timetables for trains and ferries. Rail passes for one, three or seven days allow unlimited travel on the Levanto–La Spezia stretch (including stops at all of the Cinque Terre) and the use of electric buses to the sanctuaries (boat travel is extra). From April to October, the Navigazione Golfo dei Poeti (<www.navigazionegolfodeipoeti.it>) operates a regular service (8–10 boats a day) between Monterosso and Riomaggiore (25 minutes). Boats do not stop at Corniglia. The villages can also be reached by boat from Sestri Levante, Levanto, La Spezia, Portovenere and Lerici. You can also explore the park on horseback, by horse-drawn carriage or bike. For more information visit <www.cinqueterre.it>.

into the villages and parking in most of them near impossible. Levanto to the west of the Cinque Terre makes a good base for visiting the villages. A pleasant if unremarkable resort, it has a good, long beach, ample hotels and an old quarter with a handful of historic sights.

The first of the Cinque Terre is **Monterosso al Mare**, the largest, most easily accessible and most commercialised of the five. Set on the main Paris–Genoa–Rome railway line, and with 20 hotels and well-equipped beaches, it's more of a resort than a fishing village. The old part of the town, separated from the beach by the railway line, has pleasant little alleys and a Gothic church (San Giovanni Battista) with a beautifully sculpted rose window in marble. Higher up, the Church of San Francesco, attached to a monastery, shelters paintings by Ligurian artists and a *Crucifixion* which was at one time attributed to Van Dyck.

Vernazza is perhaps the prettiest of the villages with its tightly packed houses and imposing church clustering around the small harbour. It's also hugely popular, the main street lined by pizzerias, souvenirs and bars. A narrow stairway leads up to the 16th-century castello and tower for fine views of the sea. Although there is only one fisherman left in the village, there's no shortage of seafood restaurants.

Vernazza

➤   **Corniglia**, the smallest and least visited of the Cinque Terre, is set on a rocky outcrop about 100m (330ft) above the sea. If you arrive by train, you either have to hike up the hill and climb 377 steps or wait for one of the green shuttle buses to transport you. The villagers have been producing Cinque Terre wine for over 2,000 years and every May they hold a Sciaccetrà wine festival.

Manarola vies with Vernazza as the most picturesque of the villages: a delightful conglomeration of multicoloured houses hugging the black rockface. The main street, lined by little shops selling Cinque Terre wine, slopes steeply down to the small port. You can find out about the traditions of local viticulture at the little Wine Museum (open daily 10am–6pm; free).

Last but not least is **Riomaggiore**, whose pastel-hued houses huddle on rocky slopes above the pretty little port. The national park has its headquarters here, near the station. The Via del'Amore (Lover's Lane), cut into the cliff, links the village with Manarola. The sea views are lovely, but the crowds and graffitti can detract from the romance.

Gulf of La Spezia

The beauty of the gulf inspired many a poet, from Petrarch to Shelley and Byron. Despite industrial La Spezia at its head and tourist growth around its shores, the gulf still enchants with its rugged headlands, mountain views and islands.

➤   At the end of a narrow, twisting road, set on a rocky peninsula, **Portovenere** is one of Liguria's loveliest towns. It's a ravishing sight if you arrive by boat, with its six-storey multicoloured houses wedged below the **castle** and the little **Church of San Pietro** on the tip of the windswept promontory. In the 12th century the town was fortified by the Genoese in defiance of the Pisans who had built a stronghold at **Lerici** across the bay. The houses formed a defensive wall, with trapdoors used to block stairways and alleys between them.

From the bustling waterfront, steep, narrow stairways lead up to the cobbled streets and alleys of the old town, with the charming Romanesqe **Church of San Lorenzo** and the ruined Genoese castle on the clifftop. The name Portovenere comes from an ancient temple dedicated to Venus (Venere), which occupied the promontory where San Pietro now sits. This enchanting Gothic church, built with bands of black and white marble, commands fine views of the Cinque Terre. The nearby **Byron's Grotto** (currently under restoration, also known as Grotta Arpaia) is said to

Coastline near Portovenere

have been the poet's launching pad when he swam an impressive 8km (5 miles) across the bay to visit Shelley at his villa at San Terenzo.

The seafront is strung with open-air cafés and fish restaurants, all featuring the local speciality of *muscoli* (mussels). From the port, boats depart regularly for trips around the offshore islands of **Palmaria**, **Tino** and **Tinetto**, now protected within the Portovenere Regional Nature Park. If you want to land on Palmaria, little boats will take you across via the mussel beds for a euro or two. You can lunch at the lovely Locanda Lorena *(see page 141)*, then take the walking trails over the island for views of cliffs, inviting coves and the neighbouring Isola del Tino. This smaller island preserves ruins of

La Spezia locals

an ancient abbey, but can be visited only on 13 September, the feast of San Venerio.

It is no surprise that most tourists give **La Spezia** a miss – it's a large industrial town and the biggest naval base in the country. But for the culturally inclined it is one of the best towns to visit on the Riviera. There are now seven museums, including the excellent **Museo Amedeo Lia** (Amedeo Lia Museum, Via Prione 234; open Tues–Sat 10am–6pm; admission fee). The collection of art, bequeathed by the industrialist and patron of the arts, Amedeo Lia in 1995, features 13th- to 18th-century paintings, sculpture, miniatures, archaeology and *objets d'art*. The setting is a 17th-century convent. If time is limited, concentrate on the Renaissance paintings in Room IV, and the portraits in Room VII, particularly the *Portrait of a Gentleman* by Titian, *Portrait of a Procurate* by Gentile Bellini and the *Self-Portrait* attributed to Pontormo. Further collections donated to the city in recent years can be seen in the Museum of Seals (next to the Museo Amedeo Lia) and the Centre of Modern and Contemporary Art at Piazza C. Battisti 1. Above the town, the castle houses the **Archaeological Museum** with a collection of well-preserved Copper and Iron Age statues and remains from the Roman colony of Luni. Down on the seafront, the palm-fringed promenade is backed by luxuriant public gardens and looks across to the Apuan Alps in Tuscany. The Arsenale is closed to the public but you can visit the Naval Museum by the entrance.

South of La Spezia

The coastal road south of La Spezia brings you to **San Terenzo** where in 1822 Shelley and his wife Mary Wollstonecraft, author of *Frankenstein*, rented a house called Casa Magni. It was from here that the poet took the fateful boat trip to Livorno to see Byron and to welcome the writer Leigh Hunt to Italy. On his way back, the yacht capsized in a sudden squall and the 30-year-old poet drowned.

Neighbouring **Lerici** is an attractive, lively and well-heeled centre sheltering below the well-preserved **Castello di San Giorgio** (Castle of St George). An important medieval trading centre, the town was captured from the Genoese by the Pisans in 1241, who built the castle. This was enlarged by the Genoese who took control 15 years later. Following the discovery of dinosaur tracks in the area, the castle became home to the Museo Geopaleontologico (Palaeontology Museum; open Tues–Sun 10.30am–12.30pm, 2.30–6pm, until 5.30pm in winter, midnight in summer; admission fee). Large models of dinosaurs seem incongruous, but the museum is worth visiting for the views.

In the resort, life focuses on the seafront, where fishermen still bring in the catch, cafés line the promenade, and sunseekers enjoy sandy beaches or lie on boulders.

The castle at Lerici

WHAT TO DO

SPORTS

Liguria has plenty of pursuits for the actively inclined. The 300-km (185-mile) coastline offers excellent swimming and a range of watersports, while the cliffs and hinterland are perfect for hiking or mountain biking.

Water Activities

Beaches. Swathes of golden sand are hard to come by. Beaches are mainly pebble and shingle, although private concession areas often import sand. Of the two rivieras, the Riviera di Ponente has the better beaches, especially at Alassio where there are nearly 4km (2½ miles) of soft sand. Most of the decent beaches are cordoned off into private concession areas called *stabilimenti balneari* ('bathing establishments') or *bagni*, which provide sunbeds, parasols, changing cabins and often bar, restaurant and sports facilities. Costs vary even along the same beach and are at their highest in the prestigious resorts around the Portofino Peninsula. (At Paraggi near Portofino you can expect to pay over €30 a day for a day's use of a sunbed and changing cabin; in the San Remo region the cost comes down to around €18.) The cost may depend on which row of sunbeds you are allocated; the one closest to the sea is the more expensive. Most beaches hire pedaloes, and some organise children's activities. Public, non-paying areas are normally no more than scraps of grey sand or pebble sandwiched between the regimented private areas. Some of the best swimming is off the rocks, away from the crowds. Beaches anywhere near industrial Genoa are best avoided.

Seeing the coast from the water, Camogli

Water sports. Liguria's coastline of bays and inlets and a string of smart, well-equipped marinas attract watersports enthusiasts of all kinds. Windsurfers are drawn to the Riviera di Ponente, and to Varigotti and Pietra Ligure in particular. Harbours will hire dinghies or motorboats without a licence (a 4m/13ft Boston Whaler rented from Rapallo costs around €100 for half a day) or you can hire a boat with a skipper. Around 60 diving centres are dotted along the coast, the best areas being Ventimiglia and the Portofino and Cinque Terre marine parks. Note, though, that numbers of divers are strictly controlled in the marine parks. Polo Sub (<www.polosub.it>) offer courses at all levels, equipment hire, full-day boat excursions, single dives and night dives. Many of the larger hotels and holiday villages offer their own facilities, such as water sports, beach activities, tennis, table tennis, aerobics, boat and bike hire, horse riding and special activities for children.

Land-based Activities

Hiking. Trekkers are increasingly attracted by the quiet routes and breathtaking views of Liguria's hinterland. Paths often

---

Boat Trips and Whale-watching

Hopping on ferries is a great way of seeing the eastern Riviera. The towns and villages are served by Tigullio and Golfo Paradiso services *(see page 122)*, which run regular ferries in season. Tigullio also offers whale-watching trips, departing from Genoa and several of the main towns along the Riviera di Levante. Keep in mind that there is no guarantee of spotting a whale and you are much more likely to see dolphins. From Genoa's Porto Antico, Alimar (<www.alimar.ge.it>) conducts regular 45-minute boat trips of the port, affording good views of the city from the sea. From April to September, Alimar operates an additional service to San Fruttuoso and Portofino.

Scuba diving

follow centuries-old, steep mule tracks which were built to link the inter-valley roads between trading posts. The **Alta Via dei Monti Liguri** crosses the entire province, from Ventimiglia to the meeting of the valleys of the rivers Magra and Vara near La Spezia. The route, over 400km (250 miles) long, is divided into 43 sections, with walks of one to four hours. The website <www.altaviadeimontiliguri.it> has maps and full information in English on all the trails. The paths are well marked and rated according to the level of difficulty, from 'T' for Tourist (i.e. easy) to 'EE' for expert trekkers. The route offers a superb panoramic balcony, overlooking the sea to the south, and the Alps and Po valley to the north. Further trails connect the Alta Via dei Monti Liguri to the coast, enabling you to easily join up with sections of the main route. Alpine refuges are open from the end of June to the end of September. For information, contact the Italian Alpine Club, 7/3 Galleria Mazzini, 16121 Genoa, tel: 010 592122, < www.cai.it>.

Along the coast, the favourite walks are the stunning cliff paths of the Cinque Terre *(see page 74)* and the scenic Portofino Promontory protected within the Parco Naturale Regionale di Portofino.

Mountain biking. The Cinque Terre National Park has developed mountain-bike trails of varying standards (details from Riomaggiore Information Office, tel: 0187 920633). The starting point for most excursions is the Madonna di Monte-nero sanctuary on the hill above Riomaggiore, affording breathtaking views of the gulf. A hiking centre has opened here, with some spartan guest rooms. The trails of the Alta Via dei Monti Liguri *(see page 85)* are suitable for mountain bikers as well as hikers. West of Genoa, the area around Finale Ligure is particularly popular for mountain bikers.

Serious cyclists on the road

Golf. Liguria has three 18-hole golf courses: the Garlenda Golf Club, next to the Meridiana Hotel near Albenga (tel: 0182 580012, <www.relaischateaux.com/ meridiana>), also with tennis, riding and a gym; the Degli Ulivi Golf Course, between San Remo and Monte Bignone (tel: 0184 557093); and the Rapallo Golf Course (Via Mamelli 37, Rapallo, tel: 0185 21777), with tennis and riding. Arenzano, west of Genoa, and Lerici on the eastern Riviera each has a nine-hole golf course.

Extreme sports. Fans of free-climbing are growing in number, particularly around Finale Ligure where there are 20 organised centres with numerous routes at different levels. Finale and nearby Varigotti are also centres for skydiving. Bungee-jumping enthusiasts can launch themselves from the Loreto bridge, 120m (395ft) over the Argentina River near Triora.

High divers off the rocks

Riding. Stables are dotted around the hills and mountains behind the coast. The Cinque Terre offers some of the finest pony-trekking scenery. From the Equestrian Centre at Case Pinaca above Corniglia, you can take half-day, whole-day or two-day treks; or you can hire a horse-drawn carriage with a driver. The Fattoria di Alessandra (Via Margubbio 1, 19031 Ameglia, tel: 340 8549378, <www.agriturismoalessandra.it>), on the Tuscan border, offers horse and pony holidays especially for families with young children. Guests can stay on the farm.

Skiing. During the winter, the mountain zones are often covered with snow and you can be skiing just a few kilometres from the sea. Monesi di Triora (Imperia province) has two ski lifts and slopes of varying degrees of difficulty.

Tennis. In 1878, thanks to the British, Bordighera boasted the first tennis club in Italy – and the second one in Europe after Wimbledon. Tennis clubs are still going strong. Most towns and resorts have public courts which you can hire on an hourly basis. Ask at the local tourist office for details.

San Remo Casino

ENTERTAINMENT

Genoa has no shortage of nightlife. You can find details of clubs, discos, bars with live music, wine bars and cinemas in the tourist office free guide (available at the airport and Stazione Principe).

The waterfront has its seamier side along Via Gramsci, but the alleys in the heart of the historic centre have a more inviting late-night scene with wine, tapas and cocktail bars, as well as clubs and discos. The **Teatro Carlo Felice** (Piazza de Ferrari, tel: 010 589329, <www.carlo felice.it>), rebuilt in the 1980s and 90s *(see page 37)* has made its mark again on the cultural scene, staging major opera and ballet events as well as jazz and rock concerts. The Teatro della Corte, Borgo Pila, near Stazione Brignole, hosts theatre, concerts and other cultural events, while the Teatro delle Tosse and Teatro Modena both offer alternative theatre.

The hottest spots along the western Riviera are Alassio, San Remo and Finale Marina, all of which offer clubs, discos and bars. San Remo's social life has focused on the Art Nouveau **casino** for over a century. Laying your bets can be combined with a meal at its elegant restaurant (with live orchestra) or a late night at the neighbouring Disco Loco. For the gaming rooms you need to be over 18, and produce a passport or ID. Jackets, but not ties, are compulsory for men, except in summer. Admission is €7.50 at weekends, free Mon–Thurs. Gaming rooms open at 2pm, 2.30pm or 4pm depending on the games you want to play, closing at 3am or 4am at weekends. Slot machines are open from 10am.

Along the Riviera di Levante, Portofino has some glamorous bars for the well heeled. Santa Margherita Ligure and Rapallo have a larger selection plus the occasional disco. Between Portofino and Santa Margherita Ligure, at the tiny resort of Paraggi, the stylish Carillon restaurant/nightclub continues to attract the jet set. But more often than not, nightlife along the Riviera amounts to no more than a stroll along the promenade and a nightcap in a café or bar, where you can watch the world go by.

SHOPPING

Shopping in Lerici

Not surprisingly, Genoa offers the best choice, particularly for fashions and antiques. San Remo is good too, though it's much more relaxing browsing around the small shops and boutiques in the pedestrianised old quarters of the smaller coastal towns and villages.

Markets. Many of the main towns along the coast have colourful weekly markets where you can buy anything from clothes and leather to pots of pesto and whole hams and cheese. Genoa has a bustling daily food market, the Mercato Orientale, occupying an 18th-century cloister on Via XX Settembre; San Remo has one of the best food markets of the Riviera, held on Tuesday and Friday in Piazza Eroi Sanremesi. Of the weekly markets, Ventimigia's is the largest and most popular, especially with French visitors who pop across the border to snap up bargains. Early risers will enjoy the flower market at San Remo, held Monday to Saturday 4–8am. This is for traders only, but there is nothing stopping you watching the sales. Many coastal towns have monthly antiques markets, where you can browse among handicrafts, worthless junk or genuine antiques. Bargaining (even if it's only in sign language) is always worth a try. For details of markets ask at the local tourist office.

A Pesto Recipe to Try at Home

Pesto sauce, a delicious Genoese invention, can be sampled in the region's restaurants and bought in delicatessens and at market stalls. What goes into an authentic pesto is not in doubt, but the quantity of each ingredient is hotly debated by local chefs. The following recipe, using average quantities, is good to try when you get home.

Grind two firmly packed cups of fresh basil leaves and two cloves of garlic to a paste with a pestle and mortar or food processor. Add half a cup (or less) of pine kernels, followed by a little extra virgin olive oil and half a cup of grated cheese, which stricly speaking should be 50 percent parmesan and 50 percent pecorino (either will do). Whiz until smooth and gradually add half a cup of olive oil until the desired consistency is reached. Season with salt and serve with pasta. In Camogli, the pine kernels are sometimes replaced with hazelnuts.

Food and drink. Every town has small shops and stalls selling typical Ligurian produce. You can choose from foil-wrapped bottles of Imperia olive oil (said by some to be the best in Italy), the small black olives from Taggia, local pasta such as *trenette* or *trofie*, jars of *porcini* (mushrooms) or peppers, herbs and honey. Propping up the pastas will be bottles of local wine, fruit-flavoured grappas and herbal liqueurs. In Dolceacqua you can taste and buy the local Rossesse wine from the cooperativa in the centre, and in the Cinque Terre you can find the white eponymous

Local produce in Monterosso

wine and the rarer, sweeter Sciacchetrà. It's as well to sample or buy the wines in the region in which they're produced – the production is limited and some are hard to find outside the area. The excellent Museo dell'Olivo at Imperia *(see page 52)* has a shop selling high-quality Fratelli Carli oil (unavailable elsewhere on the Riviera), along with olive oil-based soaps, cosmetics and creams and items made from olive wood. In Taggia you can visit the factory of Giuseppe Boeri, <www.olioboeri.com>, at Viale Rimembranza 34, producers of high-quality extra virgin oil made from the local taggiasca olives.

Liguria's most famous cake is the *pandolce genovese*, made with candied peel, pine kernels and raisins, similar to the *panettone* from Milan and found throughout Italy. Well

Fancy flip-flops in San Remo

known too are the *amaretti* or baby macaroons from Sassello and the *baci,* the cream-filled chocolate and hazelnut biscuits from Alassio.

Handicrafts. Most souvenirs are mass-produced, but traditional handicrafts are kept alive in a few centres. For ceramics go to Savona or Le Albisole *(see page 65);* for glass, try Altare *(see page 64).* Examples of the age-old craft of lacemaking can be found in Portofino, Santa Margherita Ligure and Rapallo. Emilio at 1 Piazza Cavour, Rapallo, sells the *pizzi al tombolo* or handmade pillow lace that wives of fishermen used to make when their men were away on sea voyages, and the town has a lace museum in its Villa Tigullio. East of Rapallo, Zoagli has been producing velvet and damask since the 16th century. The Seterie du Zoagli Cordani (Via San Pietro 21; open May–Oct Mon–Sat 9am–6pm; <www.seteriecordani. com>) is one of the few remaining family businesses, producing Jacquard velvet woven on early 19th-century looms, taffeta and organza, embroidered tulle and silk stoles, shirts and ties. Further along the coast, Chiavari is known for macramé and woodcrafts, especially chairs and picture frames.

Fashions. Genoa has the best choice for designer fashion, particularly along Via Roma and Via XXV Aprile. Via XX Settembre, the main shopping thoroughfare, has department and fashion stores. Portofino, Santa Margherita Ligure and Rapallo have no shortage of designer boutiques, but you'll find cheaper prices in less chic towns such as Chiavari and La Spezia.

CHILDREN

Children won't want to spend much time in traffic-choked Genoa, but the **Aquarium** *(see page 29)* at the Porto Antico is a sure winner. They can stroke the skates and rays, and there are seals, dolphins and sharks to feed. In the same part of town is a play and educational centre catering for those aged 3–14, La Citta dei Bambini (Kids' City; Antichi Magazzini del Cotone, Porto Antico; open July–Sep Tues–Sun 10.30am–7.30pm, Oct–June Tues–Sun 10am–6pm; admission fee).

Along the Riviera, the beaches, ferry trips and water sports are obvious attractions for youngsters. Le Caravelle water park at Ceriale, north of Albenga (<www.lecaravelle.com>, open daily June–Sept; admission fee) offers plenty of aquatic entertainment with its water slides, chutes and swimming pools.

At the Aquarium in Genoa

Festival Calendar

February San Remo: *Festival della Canzone Italiana* (song festival) – a major event in the world of Italian pop. Pieve Ligure: *Sagra della Mimosa* – colourful festival with floats created from mimosa. Taggia: *Festa dei Furgari* – celebrates the town's narrow escape from the Saracens.

March–April Genoa, Savona, Ceriana and Triora: Holy Week celebrations include processions on Maundy Thursday or Good Friday; Bordighera stages a palm procession on Palm Sunday.

May–June Baiardo: *Festa della Barca* (Festival of the Boat) – pagan ritual dance around a tree in the piazza on Whit Sunday (seventh Sunday after Easter). Camogli: *Sagra del Pesce* (fish festival).

June Genoa: Festival of San Giovanni Battista Patrono di Genova (St John the Baptist, patron saint of Genoa) – services, processions; celebrations also take place in Celle Ligure and Laigueglia, where a huge bonfire is lit and 5,000 floating candles are launched into the sea. Diano Marina and Sassello: *Corpus Domini Infiorate* – floral patterns decorate the streets.

July Genoa: International Ballet Festival. Rapallo: *Madonna di Monteallegro* – procession and fireworks. Taggia: *Festa della Maddalena* – ancient dance of fertility known as the Dance of Death

July–August Cervo: International Festival of Chamber Music. Bordighera: *Salone dell'Umorismo* – Festival of Humour.

August Ospedaletti: *Sagra du Pignurin Pan e Vin* – distribution of wine, fried fish, bread and other food. La Spezia: Festival of the Sea – regatta and fireworks. Camogli: *Festa della Stella Maris* – procession of boats from Camogli to Punta Chiappa. Ventimiglia: *Corteo Storico* – processions in historical costumes. Lavagna: *La Torta dei Fieschi* – re-enactment of the marriage of Count Opizzo Fieschi and Bianca de' Bianchi. San Remo: festival celebrating the Madonna della Costa, who saved a local sailor from drowning – fireworks, processions and feasting. San Fruttuoso: *Cristo degli Abissi* – participants dive down to a statue of Christ on the seabed.

September Noli: *Regata dei Rioni* – historical regatta and procession. Imperia: a vintage regatta is held every other year (2006, 2008, etc).

October Genoa: International Boat Show. San Remo Rally.

EATING OUT

The simple ingredients of Ligurian cuisine are the very essence of the much-acclaimed Mediterranean diet: abundant seafood, fresh fruit and vegetables and ample doses of light and delicate olive oil. Although the culinary traditions are meat- rather than fish-based, seafood now predominates, especially along the coast. Fresh herbs are key ingredients, grown everywhere, and used with fish, meat, pasta and – most famously – in *pesto genovese*. Made with basil, pine kernels, pecorino and/or parmesan cheese, garlic and copious amounts of extra virgin olive oil, this green, tangy sauce adorns numerous pasta dishes, and is added to soup to make *minestrone alla genovese*. Named after the pestle that is traditionally used to grind the basil, the sauce was invented by the Genoese as a cure for scurvy, which used to plague Ligurian seafarers on their long voyages. Nowadays you can find it in glass jars in supermarkets throughout the Western world, but nothing beats the fresh basil that has just been ground with cheese and the highly prized local olive oil.

Baiardo restaurant sign

Where to Eat

Although traditionally a *ristorante* is smarter, more professional and expensive than a *trattoria*, the difference between the two establishments these days is negligible; and often a simple homely trattoria, with red checked tablecloths and no menu, will serve the most authentic and satsifying fare; there are also very smart, pricey trattorias with international, tourist-focused menus. In general there are far more casual trattorias, wine shops, pizzerias and *foccacerie* than fancy establishments. Along the coast, you can find plenty of pizzerias doubling up as restaurants, enabling you to have a full three- or four-course meal or simply a cheap pizza. The best pizzerias have wood-fired ovens and are open only in the evenings. An *osteria,* literally a tavern or inn, can be any type of restaurant but is likely to be an older, more traditional type of place. In Genoa the *friggitorie* serve food fried in local olive oil.

Mussels in Portofino

What to Eat

The *antipasto* is the starter, which will be a seafood salad, smoked fish, cold cuts of *prosciutto* or marinaded vegetables. Next comes *il primo* – pasta, risotto or soup. *Il secondo* is the fish or meat dish (often it's fish only on Ligurian menus), followed by *il dolce* or dessert. The *antipasti* and *primi* tend to be the most tempting and appetising courses – and often the best value. No one expects you to have all four courses; these days it's normal in all but the most formal restaurants to have, say, an antipasto and a primo, or a pasta and a dessert.

Ligurian **pasta** comes in all shapes and sizes, and is served with a huge variety of seafood or stuffed with fragrant herbs. The single most popular traditional dish is *trenette al pesto*, a noodle-like pasta served with a sauce of pesto, green beans and small pieces of potato. The same sauce is served with *trofie* (little squiggles of pasta made with wheat or chestnut flour). Pesto also comes with spaghetti, lasagne, fettuccine, linguine or virtually any other pasta. Look out too for *salsa di noci*, a delicious creamy walnut sauce, often served with *pansotti* – ravioli stuffed with fresh herbs. Every menu offers a wide range of pasta with seafood sauces, typically *spaghetti alle vongole* (with small

---

Olive Oil

Ligurians (like the Tuscans and Umbrians) claim their olive oil is the best in Italy. For centuries they have been cultivating olives on the terraced slopes behind the coast. The small black olives from Taggia (called *taggiasca*) are cold-pressed to produce the best of Liguria's olive oil. It is fragrant and fruity and you can buy it directly from small family producers in the town of Taggia and the surrounding region. Look out for signs saying *'Frantoio'* (oil press). If you are buying elsewhere make sure the bottle is labelled extra virgin DOP (Denominazione d'Origine Protetta), the EU guarantee that the oil comes from a well-defined geographical area and is produced from cold-pressing methods. For the highly informative Museo dell'Olivo at Imperia, *see page 52.*

clams), or *alla scogliera* (with clams and mussels), *risotto gamberetti e asparagi* (rice with shrimps and fresh asparagus), *tagliatelle al nero di seppia* (tagliatelle with squid ink) and *linguine ai futti di mare* (noodles with seafood).

The choice of **soup** is likely to feature *zuppa di pesce*, a hearty fish soup (usually for a minimum of two), which is a meal in itself. *Zuppa di frutti di mare*, seafood soup, normally comes with clams, mussels and squid. Fish is also the main ingredient of *burrida*, a stew made with mixed fish in a tomato sauce with vegetables, anchovy fillets and pine kernels and of *ciuppin*, a fish soup similar to the French *bouillabaisse*. *Ceci* or chickpeas are key ingredients in vegetable soups such as *mesciuà* and *zimino di ceci*.

Along the coast **fish** fans are spoilt for choice. Menus are usually 80 percent fish-based. The ubiquitous anchovy *(acchiuga)* is served as a starter, either simply marinated, stuffed with herbs or baked with onions and potatoes. *Muscoli*, the local word for mussels *(cozze* elsewhere in Italy) are cooked with white wine, garlic and onion or come stuffed with fresh herbs, cheese, mortadella, tomatoes, onion, egg and wine. Mussels are abundant around the La Spezia region, where they are farmed. The local *datteri di mare,* mussels which look like dates (hence the name), are now protected and no longer available in fish restaurants. Nearby Lerici is known for *moscardi* (octopus).

> **The smaller fish are served whole at a fixed price, the larger species such as swordfish and tuna will be charged by the *etto* (100g) and it's wise to check out the price before ordering. *Grigliata mista*, simply grilled fresh fish, is usually the priciest item on the menu – and the most memorable.**

Fish served as a main course include *orata* (gilt-head bream), *tonno* (tuna), *branzino* or *spigola* (sea bass), *pesce spada* (sword-

[handwritten: Sat. lunch.]

[handwritten: Tagliatelline casalinghe ai bianchetti]

Shellfish pasta in San Remo

fish) and *triglie* (red mullet). These will come either simply grilled, lightly fried, baked or served in a marinade. The ubiquitous *orata* often comes with a sauce of black olives, pine kernels, white wine and potatoes.

The Genoese favourite of *stoccafisso accomodato alla genovese,* dried cod cooked in a casserole with olives, potatoes and pine kernels, used to be the staple diet of seafarers. But the real *tour de force* is *cappon magro*: a bed of diced vegetables piled high with six or so different fish, coated in an anchovy sauce and garnished with eggs, artichokes, shrimps, prawns, oysters and whole crayfish. Believe it or not, this was a *'maigre'* dish – reserved for a day of fasting! Today you sometimes come across it on the menus of upmarket restaurants, but it's only available if you order in advance.

Fresh **vegetables**, especially artichokes, courgettes, asparagus, leeks, chard and tomatoes, are key products of the local cuisine. They are used in antipasti and pasta sauces or

Fruit and ice-cream platter

form the bases of soups and stews. *Torta di verdure* is a vegetable pie using seasonal produce, such as chard, courgettes and onions, with fresh herbs. Look out too for *verdura ripiena,* fresh vegetables stuffed with rice and seafood. Inland, *porcini* (mushrooms) grow under chestnut trees and are cooked *alla genovese*, with potatoes, garlic and basil, or coated in breadcrumbs and fried. Another vegetable dish, *torta pasqualina,* is made with numerous layers of pastry filled with spinach, artichokes and courgettes, mixed with egg and cheese. The name means 'Easter pie', but it can be eaten at other times.

Despite the abundance of fruit produced in the region, Ligurians (like other Italians) are not great **dessert** creators. Apart from smart restaurants, desserts won't feature on the menu but the waiter will tell you what's available. The usual choice is ice cream, sorbet and perhaps a home-made tart or *tiramisù* (a rich, Venetian dessert made with sponge fingers coffee, brandy, mascarpone, cream, eggs and cocoa).

Wines and Liqueurs

The soil and steep slopes of Liguria are not ideal for viniculture. Local wines are perfectly quaffable, but those of neighbouring Piedmont (of which there are always plenty on the wine list) are more popular with wine buffs. The white wines of Liguria are more prominent than reds, the best among them being the Vermentinos and the Pigatos, both grown west of

Genoa. Though there are distinct varieties, these whites are all crisp, dry and ideal with seafood. The only notable red of the region is Rossese di Dolceacqua (DOC), which comes from vineyards in the narrow valleys behind Ventimiglia and Brodighera, close to the French border. This full-bodied wine is particularly good with red meat and cheeses. Best of all is Rossese di Dolceacqua Superiore, matured in oak casks, but not so easy to find – only 4,200 bottles are produced annually.

Cinque Terre white wine, praised and romanticised for centuries, is still produced from vines on the slopes of the five remote villages west of La Spezia. Production is more limited nowadays and the wine is undistinguished. The rarer and more expensive Sciac-chetrà is made from the same grapes as the Cinque Terre, but the fruit is left to dry on racks in the sun, producing a strong, sweet and fruity wine. Dry versions are taken as an aperitif, sweeter ones as a dessert wine or after a meal with *biscotti*.

A choice of drinks in Ventimiglia

House wine, *vino della casa*, is variable in quality but always reasonably priced. In the cheaper eateries it will be served in litre or half-litre carafes or jugs. The more sophisticated establishments will produce a hefty wine list, featuring international as well as Italian and Ligurian wines. Waiters will automatically ask if you require bottled water, either still or sparkling; but you can always ask for regular tap water *(acqua normale)*, which is perfectly safe to drink.

A good meal is usually concluded with a *digestivo* (a glass of liqueur) a choice of *amari* (bitter-sweet herb liqueurs recommended to aid digestion), *grappa* (local firewater made from grape skins) or the almond-flavoured *amaretto* or *limoncino,* made with lemons from the Cinque Terre.

To Help You Order...

A table for one/two/three, please
Un tavolo per una persona/per due/per tre, per favore
I would like... **Vorrei...**
What would you recommend? **Cosa ci consiglia?**
How much is it? **Quanto costa?**
The bill please **Il conto per favore**

And a *digestivo* for the dog...

...and Read the Menu

In addition to the regional specialities mentioned above, here are some words you are likely to encounter on Ligurian restaurant menus.

affumicato	smoked	**olio**	oil
aglio	garlic	**olive**	olives
arance	oranges	**ostriche**	oysters
birra	beer	**pane**	bread
burro	butter	**panna**	cream
carciofi	artichokes	**patate**	potatoes
cinghiale	wild boar	**peperoni**	peppers
cipolle	onions	**pesce**	fish
coniglio	rabbit	**piselli**	peas
fagioli	white beans	**pollo**	chicken
fagiolini	green beans	**polpo/polipo/**	
finnochio	fennel	**moscardo**	octopus
formaggio	cheese	**pomodori**	tomatoes
frittata	omelette	**prosciutto**	ham
fritto misto	mixed fried fish	**riso**	rice
		salsiccie	sausages
frutti di mare	seafood	**sarde**	sardines
funghi	mushrooms	**scaloppine**	thin slices of veal
gamberetti	shrimps		
gamberi	prawns	**sogliola**	sole
gelato	ice cream	**spinaci**	spinach
insalata	salad	**succo di**	
limone	lemons	**frutta**	fruit juice
maiale	pork	**uova**	eggs
manzo	beef	**verdure**	green
melanzane	aubergine (eggplant)	**vitello**	veal
		zucchini	courgettes

HANDY TRAVEL TIPS

An A–Z Summary of Practical Information

A

ACCOMMODATION

Accommodation along the Riviera is plentiful, and ranges from luxury hotels to simple bed & breakfasts and farmhouses. All hotels are officially categorised from one to five stars, or, at the very top end of the scale five-star deluxe. The stars assigned denote amenities and are no indicator of charm or atmosphere. Generally speaking, the more stars the higher the price.

The most crowded times in the Riviera del Ponente (west of Genoa) are Easter and mid-July to the end of August or any weekend from spring to autumn; in the Riviera del Levante, it's very busy from May all the way through to early October. If you are planning a couple of days in Genoa, make it a weekend, when hotels, which pack in business travellers during the week, reduce their rates to fill the rooms. If you arrive on spec, head for the local tourist office, which will book accommodation for you. Inspecting the room before committing to a reservation is always a good idea. Breakfast, which varies from a dull crusty roll to a great spread of cheese, cold meat, cereals, croissants and fruit, is normally included in the overnight room rate. Hotels usually require confirmation of a reservation, which can be done by email or fax. A deposit of one night's stay, payable by credit card, is often requested. Failure to turn up or to inform the hotel in advance of cancellation will normally incur the loss of the deposit.

The popular alternative to a hotel, especially for those wanting to stay in rural areas, is *agriturismi*. Set up by the government in the 1970s to boost the rural economy, these are farmhouses or other rural properties that rent out rooms to tourists, often with the option of eating in. Meals are communal affairs and based on home-grown produce (two-thirds of meals and beverages are supposed to be guaranteed farm produce). Many of the agriturismi are located in remote locations, well away from the hubbub of the coast. The properties vary widely in type and quality – as do the prices – and government controls are very limited. While the image may be an ancient farmhouse in the hills among olive groves and orchards, there are many that are modern, purpose-built apartments. Some are equipped for self-catering and rented out on a weekly basis in season. Recreational activities are often provided, such as hiking, horse-riding or working on the farm. It's worth learning at least a few words of Italian since some of the agriturismi owners don't speak English. Tourist offices can supply details of local establishments, or you can find information online at <www.agriturist.com>, <www.terranostra.it> or <www.turismoverde.it>. With the exception of August, you are unlikely to have problems finding rooms.

A further option is a B&B (bed & breakfast) in a private home. Like agriturismi these have become very popular over the past few years. Costs are roughly equivalent to a two-star hotel, but in general you get better value. Properties range from ancient palazzi to modern flats. For details go to <www.bbitalia.net>.

Do you have any vacancies?	**Avete camere libere?**
I'd like a single/double room	**Vorrei una camera singola**
	matrimoniale or doppia
with bathroom/shower	**con bagno/doccia**
What's the rate per night?	**Quanto si paga per notte?**

AIRPORTS

The region is served by Genoa's Aeroporto Cristoforo Colombo, 7km (4 miles) west of the city in Sestri Ponente. The airport handles charter and scheduled flights from London and other European cities, as well as flights within Italy. AMT bus No. 100, known also as Volabus, operates a half-hourly service from the airport to the city centre, from 6.15am to 11.20pm. The bus stops at the two main stations, Principe and Brignole, as well as Piazza de Ferrari in the centre. The journey takes about 30 minutes and the €3 ticket includes use of Genoa's buses, trains, lifts and funiculars for the rest of the day. A taxi from the airport to the centre costs €15. Airport services include a tourist information office, a bank with ATM machine, internet points and car-hire outlets. If you are staying in the western part of Liguria, it may be more convenient to fly to Nice airport in France, which is a short train journey from Ventimiglia. Conversely if you are staying in the far east of the region, you could consider flying to Pisa.

What time does the train/bus leave for the city centre?	**A che ora parte il treno/pullman per il centro?**

B

BUDGETING FOR YOUR TRIP

There are wide variations in price, depending where you stay and at what time of year. Prices on the Riviera di Ponente tend to be lower than those on the Riviera di Levante. In general, the best-value accommodation and restaurants are located in inland areas, away from the coastal resorts.

Taking the region as a whole, you can expect in high season to pay around €100–140 for a comfortable double with bath, €50–80 for a double in a simple hotel; a B&B costs €30–35 per person and an agriturismo €30–50 per person for half board. A good three-course meal in a restaurant without wine costs from €30, a light lunch €10–15, coffee or soft drink €1.50–2.50, beer €2–3, spirits €3.50. For those on a budget, it's worth bearing in mind that, as in the rest of Italy, coffee or drinks taken at the bar are cheaper than those served at a table. Entry fees to museums, archaeological sites and gardens vary from €1 to €6; entrance is free for EU citizens under 18 and over 65.

C

CAMPING

Liguria has around 180 designated sites. Some are huge complexes complete with pools, restaurants, shops and sports facilities. Campsites are normally open from Easter to October and are invariably packed in August. Details are available in the tourist accommodation booklets from regional tourist offices or from the internet at <www.camping.it>. The Touring Club Italiano, also has very useful information on its website (<www.touringclub.it>).

Is there a campsite near here?	**C'è un campeggio qui vicino?**

CAR HIRE (RENTAL)

Public transport along the coast is plentiful and cheap, but hiring a car is useful for touring the hills and mountains. Bookings made on the internet and paid in advance of travel work out cheaper than hiring when you arrive. In high season a small car will cost from €230 a week including third-party liability and taxes, but excluding insurance excess. Check all extras when comparing quotes from different companies.

Cars can be picked up at Genoa airport where the major car-hire companies have their outlets. Drivers must present their own national driving licence or one that is internationally recognised. The minimum age for hiring a car is normally 25. There is a small additional charge for an extra driver. Credit-card imprints are taken as a

I would like to hire a car	**Vorrei noleggiare una macchina**
for one day	**per un giorno**
for one week	**per una settimana**
I want full insurance	**Voglio l'assicurazione completa**

deposit and are normally the only form of payment acceptable. 'Inclusive' prices do not normally include personal accident insurance, or insurance against damage to windscreens, tyres and wheels. Make sure you return the car with a full tank of fuel – there are hefty refuelling charges if you fail to do so.

CLIMATE

Liguria enjoys a long, hot summer, warm spring and autumn and, thanks to the mountains, an exceptionally mild winter. The average winter temperature rarely drops below 8°C (46°F), and in the west, around Alassio and Bordighera, it's a mild 10°C (50°F). A good time to go is May and June when it's warm and sunny, the gardens are flourishing and the sea is warm. September and early October are pleasant too, with warm temperatures and waters. The hottest months are July and August when temperatures average 25°C (77°F). In August, when Italians take their holidays, the beaches are packed and many of Genoa's shops, museums and restaurants are closed. The Cinque Terre villages are busy from May to early October, especially in spring and autumn when it's cool enough for hiking. Liguria's wettest months are October, November and December; rainfall is only slight during the summer months.

CLOTHING

As in the rest of Italy, in Liguria the wearing of miniskirts, short shorts or shoulderless garments in churches is likely to cause offence. Casual clothes are the norm for eating out in most restaurants; only in very formal places, such as luxury hotels, would you need more formal attire. Take a jersey or jacket even in summer as evenings can be quite cool.

CRIME AND SAFETY

In Genoa avoid the seamier quarters of the old city at night, especially the Via di Pré and Via A. Gramsci. Wherever you are in the region, it's wise to take some simple precautions against pickpockets and car thieves. Always lock car doors, never leave valuables visible inside and preferably leave important documents and valuables in the hotel safe. Be on your guard in busy, crowded places such as markets.

I want to report a theft	**Voglio denunciare un furto**
My wallet/passport/ticket has been stolen	**Mi hanno rubato il portafoglio/il passaporto/ il biglietto**

CUSTOMS AND ENTRY REQUIREMENTS

For citizens of EU countries, a valid passport or identity card is all that is needed to enter Italy for stays of up to 90 days. Citizens of the US, Canada, Australia and New Zealand require only a valid passport.

Visas *(permesso di soggiorno).* For stays of more than 90 days, a visa or residence permit is rquired. Contact the Italian Embassy in your own country before leaving.

Customs. Free exchange of non-duty-free goods for personal use is allowed between EU countries. Refer to your home country's regulating organisation for a current complete list of import restrictions.

Currency restrictions. Tourists may bring an unlimited amount of Italian or foreign currency into the country. On departure you must declare any currency beyond the equivalent of €10,000, so it's wise to declare sums exceeding this amount when you arrive.

I have nothing to declare	**No ho nulla da dichiarare**
It's for my personal use	**E per mio uso personale**

D

DRIVING

To bring your car into Italy, you will need an international driving licence or valid national one, car registration papers, a green insurance card (an extension to your ordinary insurance, making your policy valid for Italy), a red warning triangle in case of breakdown and a national identity sticker for your car.

driving licence	**patente**
car registration papers	**libretto di circolazione**
green card	**carta verde**

Driving conditions. The Via Aurelia (SS1) skirts the coast for most of the Riviera. The alternative is the *autostrada* (motorway), the A10 from the French border to Genoa and the A12 from Genoa to the Tuscan border. Don't be confused if you also see signs for the E80 – the road is part of the Trans-European motorway system. The motorway is the best way of covering longer stretches of coast quickly, though don't underestimate the time it can take to reach the nearest access point, particularly those near large resorts and towns. Driving through the interminable and dimly lit tunnels can be tiring, but you are unlikely to be doing very long journeys: the entire coast, from the French border to Tuscany, is less than 300km (185 miles) long. You must pay a toll to drive on the motorway, but it's worth the relatively small expense to avoid the snarl-ups on the coastal road. On exiting the motorway, make sure you get into the correct lane for cash or

Are we on the right road for…?	**Siamo sulla strada giusta per…?**

credit-card payments. There are both automatic machines and kiosks with attendants. If in any doubt, head for the latter. Sign-posting on main and rural roads is quite good, but beware of reckless drivers and motorcyclists.

Traffic in and around Genoa is among the worst in Italy. The one-way streets, chaotic traffic jams and parking problems understand-ably deter foreign drivers. The city centre can easily be covered on foot, and there's good public transport from resorts along the coast.

Rules of the road. Drive on the right, pass on the left. Speed limits are 50km/h (30mph) in towns and built-up areas, 90km/h (55mph) on normal roads and 110km/h (70mph) on main highways. At roundabouts, the traffic from the right has the right of way. Seat belts are compulsory in the front and back, and children should be properly restrained. The blood alcohol limit is 0.08 percent and police occasionally make random breath tests.

Breakdowns. In case of accident or breakdown, call 113 (general emergencies) or the Automobile Club of Italy on 116. The club has an efficient 24-hour service which is available to foreign visitors.

Petrol. Petrol is readily available, though many stations close for a three-hour break over the lunch period. On main roads there are plenty of 24-hour stations with self-service dispensers accepting

I've had a breakdown	**Ho avuto un guasto**
There's been an accident	**C'è stato un incidente**
Fill it up please	**Faccia il pieno per favore**
super/normal	**super/normale**
lead-free/diesel	**senza piombo/gasolio**
Where's the nearest car park?	**Dov'è il parcheggio più vicino?**
Can I park here?	**Posso parcheggiare qui?**

euro notes and major credit cards. The majority of filling stations –
but certainly not all – accept credit cards.

Parking. In Genoa and the coastal resorts, parking, even out of season, can be a nightmare. Places like Portofino and Lerici now have
large, expensive car parks to cope with the traffic (Portofino is €16
for half a day). When space is at a premium, and particularly in the
Riviera di Levante, hotels may charge guests €10–20 a night for a
parking space. Street parking is normally controlled by meters (costing anything from €1 for 20 minutes to €1 for three hours). Some
free parking is controlled by parking discs (if you have hired a car, a
disc will be provided).

Road signs. Most road signs in Italy are international. Here are
some written signs you might come across:

Curva pericolosa	Dangerous bend/curve
Deviazione	Detour
Divieto di sorpasso	No overtaking
Divieto di sosta	No stopping
Pericolo	Danger
Rallentare	Slow down
Senso vietato/unico	No entry/One-way street
Vietato l'ingresso	No entry
Zona pedonale	Pedestrian zone
ZTL	Limited-traffic zone

E

ELECTRICITY

The electrical current is 220V, AC; sockets take two-pin, round-
pronged plugs. Visitors from the UK will require an adaptor.

EMBASSIES AND CONSULATES

Contact your country's embassy or consulate if you lose your passport, have trouble with the authorities or suffer an accident.

The British consulate in Genoa is located at 6/A Piazza G Verdi, 16121, tel: 010 574 0071. All embassies are in Rome *(see list below)*.

Australia: Via Antonio Bosio 5, 00161 Rome; tel: 06 852 721; <www.australian-embassy.it>

Canada: Via G.B. Rossi 27, 00161 Rome; tel: 06 445 981; <www.canada.it>

Ireland: Piazza di Campitelli 3, 00186 Rome; tel: 06 697 9121

New Zealand: Via Zara 28, 00198 Rome; tel: 06 441 7171; email: nzemb.rom@flashnet.it

South Africa: Via Tanaro 14, 00198 Rome, tel: 0939 068 52541

UK: Via XX Settembre 80, 00187 Rome; tel: 06 4220 0001; <www.britain.it>

USA: Via Vittorio Veneto 119/A, 00187 Rome; tel: 06 46741; <www.usembassy.it>

EMERGENCIES

The General Emergency number is 113. The following are the numbers for each emergency service:

Police: 112
Fire: 115
Ambulance: 118

Please can you place an emergency call to the…?	**Per favore, può fare una telefonata d'emergenza…?**
police	**alla polizia**
fire brigade	**ai vigili del fuoco**
hospital	**all'ospedale**

G

GAY AND LESBIAN TRAVELLERS

Homosexual couples travelling together are generally accepted, though overt displays of affection are not always tolerated in the more remote inland regions. For general information and listings of gay venues within Italy, contact Arci-Gay, <www.arcigay.it>, 2 Piazza di Porta Saragozza, 40100 Bologna, tel 051 644 7054.

GETTING THERE

By air. Direct scheduled and charter flights are available to Genoa from London and main European cities. The cheapest scheduled flights from the UK are operated from Stansted by the low-cost air-line, Ryanair. Flights depart daily in season and take two hours. British Airways flies direct from Gatwick to Genoa. Other sched-uled airlines such as Alitalia are routed via Italian mainland air-ports. Charter flights are useful for departures from regional British airports. If you are staying in the far west of the Riviera, you could fly to Nice, and hire a car or take a train or bus across the border. Several low-cost airlines operate from the UK to Nice airport. A third option, if you are staying at the eastern end of the Riviera, is to fly to Pisa.

There are no direct flights from long-haul destinations. Passen-gers from the US, Canada, New Zealand and Australia can fly to Milan and take a connecting flight to Genoa. Before making a reservation, it's worth comparing the cost of a cheap flight to Lon-don, and then a charter or flight with a low-cost airline on to Genoa.

Details of cheap flights can be found on the internet or via the airline websites:

<www.alitalia.it>
<www.ba.com>
<www.easyjet.com>
<www.ryanair.com>

By rail. Rail travel to Liguria is slow and expensive. From the UK the quickest option is to take the Eurostar to Paris, then the overnight train to Genoa (for timetables and fares, contact Rail Europe, tel: 08705 300003). Genoa's two stations, Stazione Principe and Stazione Brignole, provide a regular service to all the coastal resorts along the Riviera.

By car. The route from the UK across France and via the French or Swiss passes into Italy takes almost 20 hours. When comparing costs, bear in mind that tolls are levied on French and Italian motorways, and that drivers going via Switzerland are required to purchase a road pass, costing 40 Swiss francs, available at the border.

By ferry or boat. Genoa is a major Mediterranean seaport with ferry links to Civitavecchia (Rome), Tunisia and the islands of Corsica, Sardinia and Sicily. The port is also a major destination for cruise ships, which either depart from here or simply stop for a visit to the city on a tour of the Mediterranean.

single (one-way)	**andata**
return (round trip)	**andata e ritorno**
first/second class	**prima/seconda classe**
What's the fare to …?	**Qual è la tariffa per …?**

GUIDES AND TOURS

Local tourist offices, travel agencies and hotels can provide details of guides and tours. In Genoa a good way to familiarise yourself with the city is to take the Giro Città bus and walking tour with an English-speaking guide (contact Macramé Viaggi, tel: 010 595 9779). Buses for the tour leave from Piazza Verde by the Stazione Brignole at 9.30am daily; adult tickets cost €13, children aged 6–12 €5, under 6 free.

H

HEALTH AND MEDICAL CARE

All EU countries have reciprocal arrangements for reclaiming the costs of medical services. UK residents should obtain the European health insurance card, available from post offices or online. This only covers you for medical care, not for emergency repatriation costs or additional expenses such as accommodation and flights for anyone travelling with you. To cover all eventualities a travel insurance policy is advisable, and for non-EU residents, essential. For insurance claims make sure you keep all receipts for medical treatment and any medicines prescribed. Vaccinations are not needed for Italy, but take with you sunscreen and mosquito repellent in the summer. Tap water is safe to drink unless you see the sign *acqua non potabile*. However, many visitors prefer to copy the locals and drink mineral water.

A pharmacy *(farmacia)* is identified by a green cross. All main towns offer a 24-hour pharmacy service, with a night-time and Sunday rota. After-hours locations are listed in local papers and posted on all pharmacy doors. Italian pharmacists are well-trained to deal with minor ailments and, although they do not stock quantities of foreign medicines, can usually supply the local equivalent. If you need a doctor *(medico)* ask at the pharmacy, your hotel or consult the yellow pages. For serious cases or emergencies, dial 118 for an ambulance or head for the Pronto Soccorso (Accident and Emergency) department of the local hospital. This will also deal with emergency dental treatment.

I need a doctor/dentist	**Ho bisogno di un medico/ dentista**
Where is the nearest pharmacy?	**Dov'è la farmacia più vicina?**

HOLIDAYS

Most shops shut on national public holidays. As well as the main holidays listed below, some towns also take a public holiday to celebrate the local saint's day.

1 January	New Year's Day
6 January	Epiphany
March/April	Easter Sunday
March/April	Easter Monday
25 April	Liberation Day
1 May	Labour Day
15 August	Assumption Day (Ferragosto)
1 November	All Saints' Day
8 December	Feast of the Immaculate Conception
25 December	Christmas
26 December	St Stephen's Day

L

LANGUAGE

A few words of Italian can be useful, particularly if you are exploring villages in the hinterland. In the main coastal resorts most Ligurians speak some English, though they do not have quite the command of the language that you find in, say, Rome or Florence. If you don't speak Italian, a knowledge of French is often useful, particularly on the western Riviera.

M

MAPS

As well as town maps the main tourist offices can provide the useful *In Liguria Tourist Map*, covering the whole region. At a scale of 1:250,000, this provides as much detail as most of the maps you can buy from bookshops or newsstands. It also gives motorway infor-

mation with a plan showing all the exits, distances and motorway
facilities. However, because of the long and narrow shape of Liguria
it's hard to find a really detailed map of the region; if you're spending
a lot of time touring, it's worth buying the *Liguria Tourist Atlas*.

MEDIA

Newspapers. English and foreign newspapers are available, normally on the same day as publication.

Television and radio. Many hotels provide satellite TV with
English-language channels. On Italian TV, there are the state-run
RAI 1, 2 and 3, plus numerous commercial channels pouring out
tacky soaps, films and non-stop ads. The state-run radio stations,
RAI 1, 2 and 3, mainly broadcast news bulletins and music. Italian
radio, like the TV, has many commercial stations.

MONEY

Currency. Since January 2002 the unit of currency in Italy has
been the euro (€) divided into 100 cents. Euro notes come in den-
ominations of 500, 200, 100, 50, 20, 10 and 5; coins in denomina-
tions of 2 and 1, then 50, 20, 10, 5, 2 and 1 cents.

Exchange facilities. Banks tend to offer the best rates, followed by
post offices, bureaux de change and hotels. Some bureaux de

I want to change some pounds/dollars	**Desidero cambiare dellester line/dei dollari**
Do you accept traveller's cheques?	**Accetta travellers cheques?**
Can I pay with a credit card?	**Posso pagare con la carta di credito?**
Where is the bank?	**Dov' è la banca?**

change offer commission-free facilities, but check first that the rate of exchange is not higher than that of the banks.

Credit cards and ATMs. The major international credit cards are accepted in the majority of hotels and restaurants, petrol stations, stores and supermarkets. Some of the smaller hotels, agriturismi and B&Bs will only accept cash, and the same is true of simple trattorias. ATMs (Bancomats) are widespread, but banks take a hefty commission – it is usually better value to use cash only when essential and pay larger amounts such as restaurant bills and pricier items in shops by credit card.

Traveller's cheques. If security is a priority, traveller's cheques are your best bet. They can be used only by the purchaser, and if lost or stolen they will be refunded. The cheques can be exchanged on presentation of a passport at banks, exchange bureaux, hotels and some shops. The cheques tend to attract a high percentage of commission and sometimes a transaction fee on top.

O

OPENING HOURS

Major museums and attractions are open all day every day. Other establishments vary widely in their opening hours, but most are closed for lunch, from 12.30/1pm to 3.30/4.30pm and for one day a week, often on a Monday. Most churches are open daily from 7/8am to noon/12.30pm, and from 4/5pm to 7/8pm. In general banks open Monday to Friday 8.30am to 1pm/1.30pm, and some also open for an hour or so in the afternoon from 2.30/3pm to 4/5pm.

Normal shopping hours in Italy are Monday to Saturday 8/9am to 1pm and 3.30/5pm to 7/8pm, though some supermarkets and stores in major town are open all day. The majority of shops are closed on Sundays.

P

POLICE

The Polizia Urbana, or city police, regulate traffic and enforce local laws, the Carabinieri are the armed military police who handle public law and order, and the Polizia Stradale patrol the highways and other roads. In an emergency the Carabinieri can be reached on 112 – or you can ring the general emergency number, 113.

Where's the nearest police station?	**Dov' è il commissariato di polizia più vicino?**

POST OFFICES

Main town post offices are open Monday to Friday 8.30am–6.30/7pm, Saturday 8.30am–12.30/1pm; sub post offices Monday to Friday 8.30am–2pm, Saturday 8.30am–noon/1pm. The Italian postal service is notoriously slow – a postcard can take as long as three weeks to reach its destination, especially during the summer. For important communications, it is best to use the more expensive express system. Main post offices offer a poste restante service. Correspondence should be addressed to Fermo Posta, Ufficio Postale Principale, followed by the name of the town where you wish to pick it up. You will need some form of identification on collection. Stamps (*francobolli*) can be bought from tobacconists (with the black and white 'T' sign) as well as from post offices.

Where's the nearest post office?	**Dov' è l' ufficio postale più vicino?**
A stamp for this letter/ postcard, please	**Un francobollo per questa lettera/cartolina' per favore**

PUBLIC TRANSPORT

Bus. Within Genoa, the AMT (Azienda Mobilità e Trasporti, Piazza Acquaverde, <www.amt.genova.it>) operates the city bus services. Tickets must normally be purchased in advance and are available from tobacconists, newspaper kiosks, ticket machines or at the AMT information offices. A ticket is valid for 90 minutes, and you can use it on as many journeys as you like. It can also be used on the metro, lifts, funiculars and trains within the Genoa region. Day tickets are also available.

Although several companies run bus services along the coast, it is usually easier to take the train. Buses, however, are useful for travelling to small towns in the hinterland.

When is the next ferry/train/ bus to....?	**Quando parte il prossimo traghetto/treno/autobus per...?**
Where can I buy a ticket?	**Dove posso comprare un biglietto?**
one way/round trip	**andata/andata e ritorno**

Ferry. Along the Riviera di Levante, going by boat is the most plea-surable way of travelling. Services are extensive. For example, the Servizio Marittimo del Tigullio (<www.traghettiportofino.it>) links Rapallo and Santa Margherita Ligure to Portofino and San Fruttuoso all year round, and from May to September (weather permitting) a ser-vice operates to the Cinque Terre. The Battelieri del Golfo Paradiso service (<www.golfoparadiso.it>; tel: 0185 772091) links Genoa, Camogli, San Fruttuoso and Portofino. Alimar (<www.alimar.ge.it>) runs a catamaran service from Genoa to Portovenere (three hours) from mid-July to mid-August only, and also to Cinque Terre's Monte-rosso (four hours). Timetables can be obtained from ports and tourist offices, or you can access them at the websites given above.

Trains. Trains are operated by Trenitalia (<www.trenitalia.com>, tel: 892021 from anywhere within Italy). An excellent, reasonably priced service is provided along the coast. You can either take the slower services which stop at all the towns or the faster Intercity, Eurocity or Eurostar trains which require a supplement of at least 30 percent. Crowding is common, especially at weekends and in season when it's advisable to make a seat reservation (on some of the faster trains reservations are compulsory). Tickets must be validated in the yellow machines on the platform before boarding. Failure to do so may incur an on-the-spot fine. Tickets may be bought on the train, but at a 20 percent supplement.

For information on train travel between the villages of the Cinque Terre, *see page 76*.

Genoa has two main railway stations, Stazione Principe and Stazione Brignole, marked on timetables as Genova PP and Genova BR respectively. Frequent trains link the two, and only take five minutes. The service to Ventimiglia on the French border runs every 30 minutes, and to La Spezia, at the eastern end of the Riviera, with even more regularity. AMT and Trenitalia operate urban and suburban railways from the Genoan suburbs of Voltri to Nervi, with 11 intermediate stops and five more in the pipeline, and from

When's the next bus/ train/boat/plane for…?	**A che ore parte il prossimo autobus/treno/traghetto/ aereo per...?**
What's the fare to...?	**Quanto costa il biglietto per...?**
I want a ticket to...	**Vorrei un biglietto per...**
single (one-way)	**andata**
return (round trip)	**andata e ritorno**
first/second class	**prima/seconda classe**
I'd like to make seat reservations	**Vorrei prenotare un posto**

Pontedecimo to Brignole with five intermediate stops and one to come. Trains run every 10 minutes, and share tracks with Intercity and Eurostar Italian trains.

After many years and long delays, Genoa has a **metro** line which now has seven stations open, from Brin in the northwest to Ferrari in the centre. The section between Ferrari and Brignole is under construction. In the next phase, the metro will be extended north, with four further stations. The predicted date for completion is 2010.

R

RELIGION

Like the rest of Italy, Liguria is primarily Roman Catholic. The church still plays a major role in the community and the majority of Ligurians are still regular worshippers.

T

TELEPHONES

Calls can be made from public telephones with a pre-paid phone card *(scheda telefónica)*, costing from €5 and available from *tabacchi* or newspaper stands. Pre-paid international telephone cards (€5), available at post offices, travel agents and other outlets are incredibly good value if you are phoning abroad. You are given a PIN number which can be used from public telephones, land lines and mobiles. When phoning abroad, dial 00 followed by the country code, the city or area code (minus the initial zero) and then the number. Calls can also be made with a charge card bought from your telephone company prior to travel. This is useful for telephoning from hotels, which levy hefty surcharges on long-distance calls. The cheapest time to telephone in Italy is from 10pm to 8am on weekdays and all day Sunday. Italian area codes have all been incorporated into the numbers, so even if you are calling from the same town you are telephoning, the code needs to be included.

Mobile phones. In order to function within Italy, some mobiles need to be activated with a roaming facility. Check with your mobile phone company before leaving. If your mobile cannot receive or make calls in Italy, you can purchase a SIM 'pay-as-you-go' card (*scheda pre-pagata*) in any mobile phone shop and have a new mobile number for the length of your stay.

TIME ZONES

Italy is one hour ahead of Greenwich Mean Time (GMT).

New York	Italy	Jo'burg	Sydney	Auckland
7am	noon	1pm	9pm	11pm

TIPPING

A 10–15 percent service charge is usually included in restaurant bills, and although a tip will always be appreciated, no extra is expected. For quick service in bars, leave a coin or two with your till receipt when ordering. Taxi drivers do not expect a tip but will appreciate it if you round up the fare to the next euro.

Thank you, this is for you	**Grazie, questo è per lei**
Keep the change	**Tenga il resto**

TOILETS

Public toilets are hard to find and not always desirable, but you can always use toilets in cafés and bars. Buying a drink at the same time will be appreciated.

TOURIST INFORMATION

Most towns have a tourist office (APT), which can supply you with maps, pamphlets and details of accommodation and local attractions. Centres with no official tourist office may have a *Pro Loco* in the town hall which serves a similar purpose but is open for limited hours in summer only. To obtain information on Genoa and the Italian Riviera prior to travel contact the Italian National Tourist Office (ENIT) in your home country.

Italian tourist offices abroad

Canada: Suite 907, South Tower, 175 Bloor Street East, Toronto, Ontario M4W3R8, tel: 416 925 4882

UK: 1 Princes Street, London W1B 2AY, tel: 020 7408 1254; <www.enit.it>

US:
630 Fifth Avenue, Suite 1565, New York, NY 10111, tel: 212 245 5618
500 North Michigan Ave, Suite 2240, Chicago, Illinois 60611, tel: 312 644 0996
12400 Wilshire Blvd, Suite 550, Los Angeles, CA 90025, tel: 310 820 1898
The ENIT website for North America and Canada is <www.italiantourism.com>.

Main town/regional tourist offices

Genoa (<www.apt.genova.it>) has tourist offices at Stazione Principe (open daily 9.30am–1pm, 2.30–6pm), the airport (open Mon–Sat 9.30am–1.30pm, 2.30–5.30pm, Sun 10am–1.30pm, 2.30–5pm) and a seasonal office at Stazione Marittima.

Alassio: Via Mazzini 68, tel: 0182 647027, <www.inforiviera.it>

Bordighera: Via Vittorio Emanuele II 172/4, tel: 0184 262322

Cinque Terre e Golfo dei Poeti: <www.aptcinqueterre.sp.it>

La Spezia: Viale Mazzini 47, tel: 0187 254311

Riviera dei Fiori: <www.rivieradeifiori.org>
Riviera delle Palme: <www.inforiviera.it>
San Remo: Palazzo Riviera 1, Largo Nuvoloni, tel: 0184 59059; <www.rivieradeifiori.org>
Santa Margherita Ligure: Via XXV Aprile 2B, tel: 0185 287485; <www.apttigullio.lituria.it>
Ventimiglia: Via Cavour 61, tel: 0184 351183

Where is the tourist office?	**Dov'è l'ufficio turistico?**

W

WEBSITES AND INTERNET CAFÉS

The official Liguria tourism website (<www.turismoinliguria.it>) is a useful source of information. See TOURIST INFORMATION *(above)* for the websites of the regional tourist offices. For details of places to stay, try <www.initaly.com>.

Internet cafés are not abundant and offices offering internet access are open only during normal office hours (that is, they are closed for a three-hour lunch break and for most of the weekend). To find out the nearest internet point, ask at the local tourist office. Hotels usually offer internet access for guests, occasionally free of charge but more often than not at higher rates than those of internet cafés or offices.

Y

YOUTH HOSTELS

For details of Liguria's hostels, visit the Italian Youth Hostels Association website: <www.ostellionline.org>. To stay at a hostel, an HI (Hostelling International) membership card is required, but temporary membership is available. There is no age limit for Italian hostels.

Recommended Hotels

At the top end of the accommodation market are the exclusive hotels of Portofino, which command some of the highest prices in Italy. At the other end of the scale are the increasingly popular B&Bs (bed & breakfasts) and the now abundant *agriturismi (see page 105)*, farm houses or rural properties.

In season, hotels with their own restaurant will often insist on half board (or occasionally even full board) with stays of no less than three days. Most hotels demand a supplement for a room with a view and, on such a stunning coastline, it's usually worth paying the extra.

The symbols below are a basic guide for the price per night for a double room with bath or shower, including breakfast, service charge and taxes during the high season.

€€€€	over 190 euros
€€€	140–190 euros
€€	80–140 euros
€	below 80 euros

GENOA

Agnello d'Oro €€ *Via Monachette 6, 16126 Genoa, tel: 010 2462084, fax: 010 2462327, <www.hotelagnellodoro.it>*. Good-value three-star hotel on a pedestrianised street close to Stazione Principe. Formerly a convent, the building has been completely restructured and today the bedrooms are modern and comfortable. Top-floor rooms overlook city rooftops and the port beyond.

Bristol Palace €€€€ *Via XX Settembre 35, 16121 Genoa, tel: 010 592541, fax: 010 561756, <www.hotelbristolpalace.com>*. Generally regarded as the most desirable hotel in the city, the Bristol Palace retains the original style of the 1920s palazzo and offers elegant, plush bedrooms decorated with antiques (and many with jacuzzis). It is conveniently situated at the heart of the shopping and business quarter, but efficient soundproofing (and air conditioning) ensures a peaceful night.

Cairoli €€ *Via Cairoli 14/4, 16124 Genoa, tel: 010 2461454, fax: 010 2467512, <www.hotelcairoligenova.com>.* Well placed for visiting the attractions of the Porto Antico and the baroque palaces flanking Via Garibaldi. The Cairoli occupies two floors of a 19th-century building. An old-fashioned lift takes you up to reception on the third floor where the welcome is friendly and the atmosphere relaxed. Guest rooms are clean and modern but by no means spacious.

City €€–€€€ *Via San Sebastiano 6, 16123 Genoa, tel: 010 584707; fax: 010 586301, <www.bwcityhotel-ge.it>.* Part of the huge Best Western chain, you could be anywhere in the world at the City Hotel. But it has the distinct advantage of a quiet and very central location (a rare combination in Genoa), plus spacious rooms and excellent bathrooms. Also some great off-season deals.

RIVIERA DI PONENTE

ALASSIO

Savoia €€ *Via Milano 14, 17021 Alassio, tel: 0182 640277, fax: 0182 640125, <www.savoiahotel.it>.* Stylish hotel right on the beach on the sweeping bay of Alassio. It has a large restaurant on the beach as well as the sea-view La Prua serving regional specialities and vegetarian dishes *à la carte*. The guest rooms at the back are half the price of those with balconies over the sea. Beach facilities are not included in the room rates.

Villa della Pergola €€€€ *Via Privata Montagù 9/1, 17021 Alassio, tel: 0182 640414, fax: 0182 554969, <www.villadella pergola.it>.* Standing well above the hustle and bustle of central Alassio, this pink villa is surrounded by beautiful gardens. Built in the late 19th century in colonial style with loggias looking out to sea, it became the home of Sir Daniel Hanbury, brother of Sir Thomas (creator of Hanbury Gardens), and one of many British aristocrats residing in Liguria at the time. The present (Italian) owner opened a few of the rooms to paying guests to meet the villa's running costs. It is still sometimes referred to as Villa Hanbury, and the guest rooms are named after members of the family.

ALBENGA

Gallinara €€ *Via Piave 66, 17031 Albenga, tel: 0182 53086, fax: 0182 541280, <www.hotellagallinara.it>*. Not a very special location on a main road west of the centre, but within walking distance of the ancient town and 300m from the sea. A modern pink building, this is a friendly, family-run hotel with bar and restaurant. Guest rooms are pleasantly furnished with floral fabrics and painted woodwork.

BORDIGHERA

Villa Elisa €€–€€€ *Via Romana 70, 18012 Bordighera, tel: 0184 261313, fax: 0184 261942, <www.villaelisa.com>*. One of the most inviting villa hotels along the coast, surrounded by lush, flower-filled gardens and retaining echoes of the Riviera's heyday. The sitting rooms have touches of grandeur (chandeliers and gilt-framed mirrors), the dining room is spacious with an airy terrace, the guest rooms fresh and modern. The hotel has been in the same family for generations. It enjoys a peaceful location in the villa area of the town, a few minutes' walk up from the seafront. Facilities include an attractive swimming pool, playground and playroom, and the owner can take guests on trips to the Alps and the French Riviera.

FINALE LIGURE

Punta Est €€€€ *Via Aurelia 1, Finale Ligure, tel and fax: 019 600611/2/3, <www.puntaest.com>*. Converted from an 18th-century Genoan villa, with stunning sea views and quiet rooms. The hotel, set among olive trees, is 2km (1¼ miles) east of Finale Ligure and across the main road from the beach. Public rooms preserve drystone walls, original fireplaces and beams. Some bedrooms occupy a modern annexe nearby. Facilities include pool and solarium. Open May to mid-October.

LAIGUEGLIA

Hotel Splendidmare €€€ *Piazza Badarò 3, 17020 Laigueglia, tel: 0182 690325, fax: 0182 690894, <www.splendidmare.it>.* Converted from a 16th-century monastery, the Splendidmare is the comfiest hotel in Laigueglia. It's also one of the most central, just a stone's throw from the beach. There is still a lot of old-world charm in the downstairs salons and the medieval-style dining room. The story goes that the skeletons discovered during restoration work belonged to a British officer and his *aide-de-camp* who had been captured and imprisoned during the coastal invasions by the British in about 1800. The officer's sword is on show. Guest rooms are comparatively modern and simple in style.

NOLI

Miramare €€ *Corso Italia 2, 17026 Noli, tel: 019 748926, fax: 019 748927, <www.hotelmiramarenoli.it>.* Converted from a 17th-century building that formed part of the defences of the Noli repub-lic, the Miramare is located across the road from the beach. Décor is mostly modern and unremarkable, but many rooms have lovely sea views and the town of Noli is a delightful place to stay.

SAN REMO

Royal €€€€ *Corso dell'Imperatrice 80, 18038 San Remo, tel: 0184 5391, fax: 0184 661445, <www.royalhotelsanremo.com>.* Well-heeled Europeans have been coming to this large, luxury hotel since 1872, and it's been in the same family ever since. You can't miss the huge white building, standing above the Corso dell'Imperatrice in a large park of palms and flower-filled gar-dens. Décor is traditional with wood floors, chandeliers and spa-cious public areas, making the most of the sea views. You can swim in the beautiful heated seawater pool or at the beach across the road. Facilities include a summer garden restaurant for candlelit dinners, tennis, mini-golf, fitness room, bridge room and children's playroom.

Sole Mare € *Via Carla 23, tel: 0184 577105, fax: 0184 532778, <www.solemarehotel.com>*. If you can't afford the likes of the Royal *(see above)* this small and friendly hotel is a good budget choice, set back from the sea, and convenient for the centre. The guest rooms with modern décor are surprisingly well equipped for a two-star hotel, and some of the upper rooms have balconies with sea views. Half- and full-board terms are available.

RIVIERA DI LEVANTE

CAMOGLI

Cenobio dei Dogi €€€–€€€€ *Via N. Cuneo 34, 16032 Camogli, tel: 0185 7241, fax: 0185 772796, <www.cenobio.it>*. Very desirable hotel in parkland overlooking the sea in the fishing village of Camogli. The villa was named after an aristocratic family of doges who originally built a villa here in 1565. It was converted into a hotel in 1956 and retains the 17th-century chapel, built for visiting priests and cardinals. Terraces, pool and spacious, airy rooms have panoramic views of the Gulf of Camogli. There are two restaurants, one overlooking the sea, the other on the small private beach.

CINQUE TERRE

Ca dei Duxi €€ *Via Colombo 36/Via Pecunia 19, Riomaggiore, tel and fax: 0187 920036, <www.duxi.it>*. A small *locanda* with simply furnished rooms in a restored 18th-century house. A few of the original features such as exposed beams have been preserved, and the breakfast room was transformed from an ancient cellar where the renowned local Sciacchetrà wine was produced. Three family rooms and three apartments to rent are also available. Private parking (extra cost) should be reserved in advance.

Da Cecio € *Via Serra 58, Corniglia, tel: 0187 812043, fax: 0187 812138*. Tiny, stone-walled inn just outside the smallest of the

Cinque Terre villages. Guest rooms are simply furnished, most with good views and all with their own bathrooms. Ligurian specialities are served in a wood-beamed restaurant, with a pretty terrace for al fresco meals. The cuisine is good home-made fare in the Ligurian tradition, but not at give-away prices.

Marina Piccola €€ *Via Birolli 120, 19010 Manarola, tel: 0187 920103, fax: 0187 920966, <www.hotelmarinapiccola.com>.* A lovely spot to start or end the day, when all the Cinque Terre hikers have gone home. The small hotel lies right on the enchanting harbour at Manarola and comprises two buildings, one just behind the waterfront with the reception/sitting area, the other with a popular restaurant right on the port with the fishing boats below. There are guest rooms in both buildings, now all with TV and air conditioning. The hotel is open all year; it's hugely popular from May to the end of October, so book well in advance. Half board is compulsory in season.

LERICI

Hotel Diora Park €€ *Via Doria 2, 19032 Lerici, tel: 0187 967124, fax: 0187 966459, <www.doriaparkhotel.it>.* Long-established family hotel set among olive trees just above the village. The centre is a couple of minutes' walk down the hill through the alleys of the old town (by car it takes longer and you can't park in the centre). The hotel has great views of the port and Gulf of Poets and it's well worth splashing out on one of the sea-view rooms. If none is available you can enjoy the scene from the bar or restaurant terrace. Specialising in fish, the cuisine is some of the best in the region, and the lavish buffet breakfasts (served all morning, from 6am to noon) have won awards. Bedrooms are prettily furnished in pale hues and floral fabrics.

LEVANTO

Stella Maris €€€€ *Via Marconi 4, 19015 Levanto, tel: 0187 808258, fax: 0187 807351, <www.hotelstellamaris.it>.* A little gem of a hotel converted from a 19th-century villa and decorated with frescoes, chandeliers and antiques. In the centre of Levanto it's 100m from the sea and just a short train trip to the Cinque Terre. Apart from the eight rooms in the main villa, there are seven others in a nearby modern annexe.

PORTOFINO

Splendido €€€€ *Salita Baratta 16, 16034 Portofino, tel: 0185 267801, fax: 0185 267806, <www.orient-expresshotels.com>.* Renowned for its roll call of the rich and famous and rated by some as the best hotel in Italy (at €1,334 a night for a sea-view double room in summer you might expect it). The monastery that once stood here fell victim to Saracen raids and was left abandoned until the 19th century when it became a private summer villa. In 1901 it was transformed into the Grand Hotel Splendido. No expense has been spared, and restaurants and pool terraces have glorious views of the bay. Facilities include a heated outdoor swimming pool, tennis courts, and a health and wellness centre. A slightly cheaper alternative is the sister hotel, the Splendido Mare, in the heart of Portofino, where guests can take advantage of all the facilities of the Splendido.

PORTOVENERE

Royal Sporting €€€€ *Via dell'Olivo 345, 19025 Portovenere, tel: 0187 790326, fax: 0187 777707, <www.royalsporting.com>.* Modern, well-equipped hotel overlooking the Gulf of Poets. An underpass gives direct access to the beach, but if you prefer to stay in situ you can swim in the seawater pool and relax in the solarium. Facilities include a tennis court, garden and small play area.

SANTA MARGHERITA LIGURE

Hotel Fasce €€ *Via Luigi Bozzo 3, 16038 Santa Margherita Ligure, tel: 0185 286435, fax: 0185 283580, <www.hotelfasce.it>.* You receive a warm welcome at this immaculate little hotel. The manageress is a mine of information about the region and will happily help you plan your day. Spotless guest rooms are well equipped for the two-star category: flat-screen TVs, laundry service, and tea- and coffee-making facilities. For breakfast, eggs and bacon can be made to order at no extra cost. The hotel is peacefully set off a main road leading down to the town centre and seafront. The hotel lacks a restaurant, but there are plenty of eateries within five minutes' walk – and if you fancy going further, bikes are lent out free of charge. Although parking is available (at extra cost), you don't need your own wheels to explore the resort or coast along here.

Villa Gnocchi €€ *Via Romana 53, San Lorenzo della Costa, 16038 Santa Margherita Ligure, tel and fax: 0185 283431, e-mail: <roberto.gnocchi@tin.it>*. A quiet little hideaway, high above Santa Margherita Ligure, and a far cry from the average coast hotel. Roberto Gnocchi, who runs it, is a great cook, an accommodating host and a valuable source of information for the region. He inherited two dilapidated farmhouses, restored the rooms and retained the family period pieces. The atmosphere is homely and rustic. Dinners are taken on the terrace, overlooking the rooftops of Sant Margherita Ligure and the Gulf of Tigullio beyond. A steep path takes you down to the centre of the resort in about 15 minutes. By car it's about 3km (2 miles). If you arrive by train, Roberto will pick you up from the station. Advance reservations are essential in season, especially for rooms with a view. Closed mid-October to Easter.

SESTRI LEVANTE

Hotel Helvetia €€ *Via Cappuccini 43, 16039 Sestri Levante, tel: 0185 41175, fax: 0185 457216, <www.hotelhelvetia.it>*. The Helvetia couldn't have a lovelier setting, overlooking the sandy crescent of the Baia del Silenzio (Bay of Silence) away from the hubbub of the centre. The hotel is casually stylish and makes the most of the charming views from the terraces and rooftop solarium. Prettily furnished guest rooms have garden or sea views. Buffet breakfasts are served on the bay-view terrace. The centre is only a couple of minutes away, but bikes are lent out free of charge if you want to explore further.

Recommended Restaurants

The recommendations below range from hole-in-the-wall pizzerias to elegant upmarket restaurants. Opening times are normally 12.30–3pm for lunch *(pranzo)* and 8pm or later for the evening meal *(cena)*. Traditionally, lunch is the main meal of the day, though this is gradually changing, particularly in Genoa and the main towns. A cover charge *(pane e coperta)* of €1–3 per person and service charge of 10–15 percent will normally be included in the bill. Where service is not included, it is normal to leave a tip. A *menu turistico* or *menu a prezzo fisso* (fixed-price menu) will normally be a three-course meal with service, cover and often wine, beer or a drink included in the set rate. More gourmet establishments may offer a *menu degustazione* ('tasting menu'), enabling you to try out a whole range of local specialities. Booking a table is advisable at the popular resorts, especially in season or at any weekends or public holidays.

The prices indicated below are a basic guide for a three-course evening meal per person, including cover charge and service, but excluding wine.

€€€€	over 45 euros
€€€	30–45 euros
€€	20–30 euros
€	under 20 euros

GENOA

Da Genio €€ *Salita San Leonardo 61/r, tel: 010 588463.* A long-established trattoria on a stepped alley near Piazza Dante. The décor is nothing special, but the place draws the locals for its home cooking and lively atmosphere. Ligurian classics include stuffed anchovies, *trofie* (pasta) *al pesto*, *torta di verdure* (vegetable pie), *stoccofisso genovese* (fish stew made with dried cod) and meat dishes served with local olives and pine nuts. The dessert menu is more elaborate than most, featuring, say, apple tart or chocolate pudding, as well as the usual ice cream and sorbet.

Da Maria € *Vico Testadoro 14r (just off Via XX Aprile), tel: 010 581080.* Students, white-collar workers and in-the-know tourists literally rub shoulders in this staggeringly cheap, humble trattoria. The set menu is under ¤10 and is likely to feature filling soups and pastas, with a simple meat or vegetarian dish, and a half litre of house wine. The setting is about as simple as you get, with long tables, red-checked tablecloths and the menu scribbled on pieces of paper. Tucked away in a narrow alley near the Piazza delle Fontane Marose, you can recognise Da Maria by the tablecloths strung out in the street to dry. Open for lunch only, closed Sun.

Da Vittorio €€–€€€ *Via Sottoripa 59r, tel: 010 2472927.* The swordfish, sea bream, live lobsters and other seafood on display are likely to lure you into this small restaurant under the Sottoripa arcades. Lobsters are a speciality; you can either splash out and have them simply grilled, or order a seafood pasta such as lobster *linguine* or have them in a delicious fish omelette. Alternatively try the *antipasto di mare misto* (mixed seafood starter) or *risotto al mare* (seafood risotto). Being near the Porto Antico, it's a popular place and you may have to queue for a table.

Gran Restoro € *Via Sottoripa 27, tel: 010 2473127.* Not so much a restaurant as a hole-in-the-wall deli, with an amazing choice of sandwich fillings. Take your pick of smoked hams, cheeses, salami or wild boar and enjoy your snack with a glass of wine or beer. Takeaway is also available. Be prepared for long queues at lunchtime. Open 7am–7pm.

I Tre Merli €€€ *Vico Dietro il Coro della Maddalena 26r, tel: 010 2474095.* This is an old *cantena* (wine cellar) converted into a fashionable wine bar. Stone walls and brickwork set the scene for full meals, pasta dishes or platters of cheese and salami. For wine buffs, there are 300 wines to choose from, including an excellent range of Piedmonts. The location is just off Via Garibaldi, the most elegant street in the city, and convenient for visiting the palazzi and galleries. It's also good for post-theatre dinners – the late opening hours (until 1am) are a rarity in Genoa.

Mario Rivaro €€€ *Via del Portello 16r, tel: 010 2770054.* Prime location off the Via Garibaldi and popular with local bankers at lunchtime. The cuisine is Genovese and the setting nautical, with wood-panelled walls lined with bottles of wine and liqueurs. *Antipasti* and *primi* (starters) include fresh anchovies, *zuppa di pesce alla Ligure* (fish soup with muscles, clams and octopus), *trofiette genovese* (pasta with pesto, potato and beans) and *pansotti in salsa noce* (ravioli-like pasta with a creamy nutty sauce). Main courses include the local speciality of *stoccofisso alla genovese* (dried-cod stew), steak in wine sauce or grilled meats. The Enrico Serafino house red is excellent value.

RIVIERA DI PONENTE

ALASSIO

La Scogliera €–€€ *Lungomare Ciccione 45, tel: 0182 642815.* Popular spot for its seaside atmosphere and range of food from snacks and crêpes to full meals. Seafood predominates and you can select from hot and cold buffets. In the evenings there are weekly barbecues and, at weekends, occasional live music. The restaurant forms part of one of Alassio's *bagni* or bathing establishments which also offers water sports and other beach facilities.

BORDIGHERA

Il Tempo Ritrovato €€€ *Via Vittorio Emanuele 144, tel: 0184 261207.* Located on the busy main street of Bordighera, this is popular with locals for its serious wine list featuring over 100 varieties, and for the simple, freshly prepared dishes. Only three or four pastas and main courses are offered daily; these are likely to feature organic, homemade pasta, local fish or Ligurian-style rabbit with white wine and olives. Friendly atmosphere and simple décor with bottles lining lemon-coloured walls. Closed Sun and Mon; lunch in summer.

Osteria Magiargé €€–€€€ *Piazza G. Viale, Bordighera Alta, tel: 0184 262946.* Bordighera is spoilt for choice when it comes to restaurants. Most of the well-known ones are in the main resort, this one is picturesquely set in Alta Bordighera, the charming old town on the hill behind. Vaults and red Venetian walls are the setting for carefully prepared fish soups, pastas with seafood and casseroled Ligurian rabbit. The extensive wine list has over 600 varieties, and there's a nearby wine bar owned by the same organisation. Tables are laid outside in summer. Reservations recommended. Closed Mon and Tues lunch.

DOLCEACQUA

Agriturismo U Fundu €€ *Via Doria, tel: 0184 206784.* Medieval dining room in the historic centre. There's a good-value four-course set menu which features typical local dishes such as *brandacujun* (salt cod and potato purée) or baked gigot of lamb. Try the Rossese di Dolceacqua wine for which the region is famous.

SAN REMO

Paolo e Barbara €€€€ *Via Roma 47, tel: 0184 531653.* This well-known restaurant is named after the husband and wife owners and chefs, Paolo and Barbara Masieri. Paolo was the youngest Italian chef to receive a Michelin star in 1989, and the restaurant has maintained its ranking ever since. The setting on a traffic-clogged street lacks charm, and there is no balcony or view; but the food is exceptional. The emphasis is on top-quality fresh ingredients, whether it's the fish just caught in the family-owned boat, the lambs or goats from local pastures or the home-grown artichokes, courgettes and melons. In an elegant traditional setting, among pastoral murals, you can tuck into exquisite *calamaretti* (baby squid) with a purée of courgettes and leeks, tartare of tuna with raw shrimps, ravioli stuffed with wild herbs and tossed in a ricotto pesto, or Ligurian specialities such as *stoccofisso* or *brandacujun*. Barbara Masieri, who is the pastry chef, creates mouth-watering made-to-order desserts. Closed Wed and Thur. Reservations advisable.

VENTIMIGLIA

Balzi Rossi €€€€ *Piazzale De Gasperi, Ponte San Ludovico (8km/5 miles west of Ventimiglia), tel: 0184 38132*. Elegant and comparatively formal restaurant just by the French–Italian border near the caves of the same name. Save it for a special occasion. It's one of the Riviera's top (and most-expensive) restaurants, popular with French as well as Italians. Not surprisingly, French influence comes into play. Closed Mon, Tues lunch, also Sun lunch in high season.

RIVIERA DI LEVANTE

CAMOGLI

La Camogliese €€€ *Via Garibaldi 78, tel: 0185 771086*. Camogli's waterfront is packed with cafés, bars and pizzerias. This is one of the most inviting eateries – a proper restaurant, jutting right out over the pebble beach and serving a tempting array of seafood. A starter of *zuppa di muscoli e vongole* (muscle and clam soup) or one of the many pastas with seafood can be followed by mixed-grilled fish or bass, bream or lobster.

CINQUE TERRE

Gambero Rosso €€€–€€€€ *Piazza Marconi 7, Vernazza, tel: 0187 812265*. The setting alone – right on the photogenic harbour of Vernazza, with tables on the waterfront – makes the restaurant one of the most sought-after in the Cinque Terre. The popular four-course *degustazione* (tasting) menu enables you to try out the local fish-based specialities; off the *à la carte* menu there is home-made *trofie* pasta with pesto sauce, *pansotti* pasta filled with ricotta and pesto, and stuffed muscles and anchovies with tomatoes and potatoes. *Mesciuà*, a local soup of beans, wheat and chickpeas, is a meal in itself. Closed Mon.

La Lanterna €€ *Via San Giacomo 10, Riomaggiore, tel: 0187 920589*. Small, friendly restaurant with a seductive setting overlooking Riomaggiore's port and some of the best seafood and pasta in the Cinque Terre. Booking is advisable at this very popular place, especially if you want a seat on the terrace at lunchtime. From the station it's a two-minute walk, via the tunnel. Closed Tues.

La Scogliera €€ *Via Birolli 103, Manarola, tel: 0187 920747.* On the road going down to the port, La Scogliera is a relatively new and very welcoming restaurant, converted from a 400-year-old ex-wine cellar. Anchovies with lemon, carpaccio of smoked swordfish, octopus soup, ravioli with salmon, and linguine with seafood, bass and beam are just a few of the numerous seafood dishes you can try here. All to be washed down of course with Cinque Terre wine.

Osteria a Cantina de Mananan €€ *Via Fieschi 117, Corniglia, tel: 0187 821166 and 0187 812320.* Tiny eatery in old cellars, with tightly packed tables and the menu on a blackboard. There are no views or terrace, just wonderful homemade bread, pesto and pasta, delicious fish and traditional Ligurian dishes, all using the freshest of produce. It's hugely popular and reservations are recommended. Remember your phrase book – very little English is spoken here.

PALMARIA

Locanda Lorena €€€ *Via Cavour 4, Isola Palmaria, Porto-venere, tel: 0187 792370.* You have only to call the Lorena from Portovenere and they will come and fetch you by boat (free of charge) for lunch. Alternatively a ferry or one of the little boats will take you across for a couple of euros. It's certainly worth it for the excellent seafood and the romantic location, with great views across the water to Portovenere. The set menu is likely to offer lobster, mussels, prawns, anchovies and squid followed by pasta with seafood, and grilled or baked fish. The Lorena has simple (but not cheap) rooms should you decide to stay. Closed Wed off season.

PORTOFINO

Ristorante Puny €€€€ *Piazza Martini dell'Olivetta 4–5, tel: 0185 269037.* If you can afford to wine and dine in Portofino, this (despite its name) is one of the best bets. By lunching or dining on a terrace table it would be hard to find a more pleasant way of absorbing

Portofino's lovely piazzetta and port. The emphasis is on fish, either as an antipasto, with homemade pasta, or or perhaps baked with bay leaves, potatoes and olives. Among the local specialities are *moscardini al forno* – baked octopus with lemon and rosemary in tomato sauce. There are occasional exotic diversions from Ligurian fare, such as *risotto al curry e gamberi* (shrimps with curried risotto). Reservations essential. Closed Thur.

PORTOVENERE

Trattoria La Marina €€ *Piazza Libertà 1, tel: 0187 790076.* One of a string of fish restaurants on the seafront of Portovenere. Try to get one of the tables outside – a good people-watching spot with lovely views across to the island of Palmaria. Worth trying are the *antipasti di mare* (seafood starter), the pasta with seafood, the grilled local fish, or the mussels which come fresh from the beds across the water.

RAPALLO

Elite €€ *Via Milite Ignoto 19, tel: 0185 50551.* Long-established family-run restaurant up from the port, offering better value than those on the seafront. *Antipasti* of smoked swordfish, *coquille St Jacques* or filet carpaccio can be followed by pasta with lobster, scampi or pesto, then to follow grilled fish, steamed bass, lobster or *sinfonia di mare* (symphony of the sea). But meat-lovers won't feel neglected here. There is veal Ligurian-style along with six different steaks, including Chateaubriand (minimum of two people) and tournedos Rossini. Closed Wed.

SANTA MARGHERITA LIGURE

Il Faro €€ *Via Maragliano 24A, tel: 0185 286867.* Family-run trattoria which greets you with a complimentary glass of Prosecco and a small *hors d'oeuvre*. The three-course set meal is good value, or off the *à la carte* menu you might be tempted by the marinaded swordfish, the homemade pasta with lobster, or the grilled bream or sea bass. In summer, tables are laid out at the back, under the portico in the square. Closed Tues.

INDEX